TWO SILVER TRUMPETS

COUPLES IN MINISTRY

Includes 30 devotions to enhance your marriage and ministry

Denise S. Millben

Two Silver Trumpets

All Scripture taken from the New King James Version® unless otherwise noted. Copyright © 1982 by Thomas Nelson. Used by permission. All rights reserved.

Scripture taken from the New King James Version®. Copyright © 1982 by Thomas Nelson. Used by permission. All rights reserved.

The Authorized (King James) Version of the Bible ('the KJV'), the rights in which are vested in the Crown in the United Kingdom, is reproduced here by permission of the Crown's patentee, Cambridge University Press.

Copyright © Denise S. Millben
P.O. Box 1945
Muncie, IN 47308
www.bridge-to-life.net
All rights reserved.
ISBN-13: 978-0997604306

TABLE OF CONTENTS

Prologue   6

Chapter 1
The Making of the Trumpets   16

Chapter 2
What Do I Bring To This Marriage?   31

Chapter 3
That's His Ministry   53

Chapter 4
His Friends, My Friends, Our Friends   62

Chapter 5
Christian Marriage   72

Chapter 6
Simply Trusting   83

Chapter 7
The Common Enemy   99

Chapter 8
Knowing   108

Chapter 9
Silence is NOT Golden   116

Devotions for Couples in Ministry

Foreword		131
1	A Servant's Heart	134
2	Speak It & Believe It	137
3	I Am	140
4	Abundant Life	142
5	Compassion	145
6	His Special People	148
7	Be Still	151
8	Benefits	154
9	Handpicked	157
10	Will God Get the Glory?	160
11	Good Shepherd	163
12	God's Goodness	166
13	Ascension	169
14	He Has Not Forgotten You	172
15	Wait For It	175
16	Truth Trumps Facts	178
17	Prepare Your Heart	181
18	Laugh	184
19	My Answer Is Yes	187
20	The Greatness in Silence	190
21	I Made It	193
22	Direction	196

23	Take A Stand	199
24	A Cry of Faith	202
25	Gracious Dealings	205
26	Get On Fire	208
27	Restoration	211
28	Wait On Him	214
29	God Our Avenger	217
30	The Land Of Faith	220

Denise S. Millben

This book is dedicated to my father

Mr. David E. Foster

1919-1987

&

My beloved husband

Bishop Stephen Michael Millben

Acknowledgments

I want to thank our heavenly Father who inspired me to write this book.

Special thanks to my husband who is my best friend. Your support during our marriage has been unrivaled. Thank you for allowing me to be transparent with our lives.

Thank you to my wonderful and helpful family.

Thanks to Mrs. Jean Webb for typing this book and Kizmin Millben Jones for editing and publishing this book and designing the cover. Without your assistance this book would not be realized.

Prologue

Marriage as God intended has been redefined by man but that does not mean that God has redefined marriage. The word of God is the standard for marriage. How can man decide to ignore the word of God and reestablish the basic framework of our nation and culture? God established marriage in the beginning. Marriage God's way is a blessing, but not without challenges. Married couples in ministry have the normal challenges of life. They must deal with issues regarding friends, family, bills, and work, but they also have the additional challenges of ministering to and counseling people when, in fact, they may need some help themselves. Many couples need additional outside assistance to help them navigate through the traps, pitfalls, victories and successes of their own lives.

This book presents practical instructions for couples in ministry. It addresses situations and circumstances that these unique couples face. The transparency of this book will allow you to peek into the lives of some real people to hear their ministry stories and observe the ways in which they deal with the problems they face in their everyday lives.

Some lessons are only learned from personal experience, but others may be gleaned from the experiences of others. It is my prayer and goal that this book will allow you to take a glimpse into the lives of others in order to learn valuable lessons the easy way. As a minister's wife for many years, I am writing this book to offer help and guidance through the rough topography of marriage and ministry. By listening to these stories you will understand that you are not the only one going through something. You have brothers and sisters who have been down this road and made it through victoriously. Therefore, this book will bring you HOPE.

The life of a trumpet is not really much different than that of any other person in the beginning. First you must be sure of your relationship with the Lord Jesus Christ. If your relationship with the Lord is shaky, your upward movement in Him will be hindered.

Let me tell you a story about a youth pastor. He was well liked and very influential with the youth. Young people felt free to go to him for advice and counsel at any time. Eventually he married, but his wife began to feel ineffective in ministering to young people because they did not freely share their concerns with her as they did with her husband. She allowed this attitude to fester in her heart without sharing her feelings with anyone. After a while, she found herself trying to compete with her husband. She would approach people and ask them to pour out their hearts to her. She even shared her own personal stories in order to get them to trust her. When this tactic backfired she told them that they need not bother her husband with their problems and that she was available to hear their concerns. Unfortunately, instead of attracting young people, she alienated many who began to think that she was speaking the sentiments of her husband. As a result, her insecurity caused great problems in the ministry. Her husband could not understand the change in the attitude of the youth. When her husband found out what she had been doing, he began to question her motives. She tried to defend herself, but her actions severely endangered their marriage for quite some time. She eventually brought her damaged emotions before the Lord and allowed Him to heal her pain. Through wise counsel, the couple was able to repair the damage and move forward in the ministry. The wife found her place in their joint ministry and they are now working together for God.

There will be times when you too will question things in your life. You should not, however, ever question your love for God or your desire to serve Him with all your heart. This matter must be settled in your heart. It is OK not to know the plan of God. That is why we walk by faith. I have said on many occasions that I felt like I didn't know anything except that I loved the Lord and would serve Him until I died. That's all I know, but the rest of my life, I haven't always been sure about.

Very early in my life I wondered if I was supposed to even go away to school. I tried to stay at home and go to school in Chicago because that was a safe place. Everything was familiar, but that was not God's plan for my life. Sometimes I would think that I finally had worked out a plan and was ready to move forward. I would move in that direction for a while only to discover that God had evidently changed His mind about me. There I was standing in the dark wondering what to do next. These times were the beginning stages of my walking by faith and not by sight.

I was the only girl in my family along with two brothers and my two loving parents. My life was fairly easy as I look back on it now. We did not have a lot of money, but we always had an appreciation for nice things. Our home was modest but comfy. If things were not perfect, I wasn't aware of it. There were five years between me and my oldest brother. He and I had a closeness that we maintain to this day. There was some sibling rivalry, but our lives were filled with love. He tells me now that he was very sad the day my husband and I got married. It was like he lost his best friend. My younger brother and I are close as well. I'm thirteen years older than him so our relationship was very different growing up but as we have grown older we have also grown progressively closer.

My school days were uneventful. I spent most of my time at church or with church members. When it came time to graduate I wanted to attend a college in Chicago. I applied and was accepted. Boy o' boy what an eye opener for me. I realized that I was not ready for the things that I saw and heard in college. I asked my father if I could drop out. He was not happy with that and discouraged me from quitting during the first semester. He said that if I finished the first semester then I could quit and go to work, which I did. I worked for the rest of that year and then began hearing about a Bible School that was located in Columbus, Ohio. I understood how Elizabeth must have felt when she heard that Mary was pregnant with Jesus---the baby leaped in her womb. When I heard about Aenon Bible College, something leaped in me and I knew that was the school I was supposed to attend.

The day finally arrived when I left the familiar and went to the unknown. That was a scary move for me. My dad took me to school and I was terrified. I did not know anyone and very few students had arrived by the time I had. I was taken to a dorm room with no one there but me. As I watched my father drive away I wanted to scream for him to come back and get me, but I sat in silence and quietly cried. In the days following, each one got progressively better. I went on to develop friendships that have lasted to this day. The school was nothing to look at aesthetically, however the staff and the students were some of the most dedicated people I had ever met. They really impacted my life and I shall forever be grateful to God for the wonderful, godly friendships that were established during the three years I attended Aenon Bible College.

One person stood out to me among the students there. He was a very nice young preacher by the name of Michael Millben. He was a very dedicated young man and was serious about his work for the Lord. I would observe him in the prayer meetings, and one time as he was sharing with the group in our chapel service he began to cry. That really touched me and showed me that he was a man that had the heart of God. We began to share our stories and reasons for coming to this school. I knew his coming there was of God. He was a very intelligent young man and had already attended a university with a plan to become a dentist and go into practice with his father. I could not believe he was willing to give up that dream and prestige to come to a school in Ohio to learn about God's word. This was remarkable to me.

We had our tests and trials at Aenon. One time I was so discouraged that I was going to call my father and tell him I was leaving and returning home. Michael and I talked about this for a long time and, after talking to him and praying together, I decided stay. Even early in our lives, I knew there was something special about this young man. At that time, I had no idea that I was going to fall in love with him and become his wife. As time went on, our friendship deepened and we did fall in love with each other. I immediately sought God because the worst thing someone in ministry can do is to marry the wrong person!

The tests came and many were in the form of other young ladies who expressed romantic interest in Michael. Jealousy is a cruel and terrible thing. It causes people to say things that hurt and to do things that can scar you forever. There were people that had made it a goal in life to break Michael and me up. To comfort me, the Lord would awaken me in the night and give me encouraging words; things that were too wonderful to have come from Satan. He would sustain this relationship through His

Word. God revealed His Word to me in incredibly new ways. Sometimes the Lord would just give me a thought and I would write it down on tissue without turning on the lights. I viewed this as God's way of turning my attention away from the negative, away from the words that bring death, unto His life giving Word. Whenever you are facing great obstacles run to the Word of God. You will be blessed if you do. In the morning, I would try to read my indecipherable scratching to no avail but the thoughts would stay with me for a long while. Eventually, I would have an opportunity to share them with someone and they would tell me that what I had shared was exactly what they needed for that particular situation in their life. I would simply reply, "To God be the glory", and keep on moving. This began to happen more and more in my life. I could say that the call was always there, but the more I yielded to God, the more He developed me into the image of what my "trumpet" should look like and sound like. The only words that will stand are the ones that come from God.

Michael, on the other hand, was a very smart young person and had ambitions to become a dentist, following in his father's footsteps. As one of the top students in his high school class, he had many things going for him. He was well liked and well known in his hometown of Jackson,

Michigan. He was a very studious young man and learning came easy to him. When he turned his life over to the Lord, he was sincere in his commitment, and the Lord called him to the ministry early in his Christian walk.

He went to the University of Minnesota for one year and while there, his academics were outstanding. He maintained a grade point average of 3.75. His course of study was to lead him into the medical field. However, the Lord had another plan for his life.

While home for the summer break after one successful year at the university, he volunteered to take an elderly gentleman to a doctor's appointment in Ann Arbor, Michigan. While he was sitting in the waiting room reading his Bible, a janitor came up to him and began asking him about the Bible. As the conversation continued, the stranger asked Michael what his plans for the future were. Michael told him that he was planning to attend a Bible College in the fall. Upon hearing that, the gentleman asked him if he had ever heard of Aenon Bible College in Columbus, Ohio. Mike said, "No." This man shared with him about the Bible College and it piqued Michael's interest. When he returned home he asked his mother if she had ever heard of that school. She had actually dated the nephew of the school's founder! Even though Michael was all set to enter a Bible College in

Minnesota, he and a friend went to Columbus to see what Aenon was like and to check out the President's church. When he arrived in Columbus, he felt the leading of the Lord to enroll at the College. As God would have it, this happened to be the same year that I also enrolled. God is frequently busy bringing us to an "expected end".

1

The Making of the Trumpets

The title, Two Silver Trumpets is taken from the book of Numbers 10:1-10.

And the LORD spoke to Moses, saying: 2 "Make two silver trumpets for yourself; you shall make them of hammered work; you shall use them for calling the congregation and for directing the movement of the camps. 3 When they blow both of them, all the congregation shall gather before you at the door of the tabernacle of meeting. 4 But if they blow only one, then the leaders, the heads of the divisions of Israel, shall gather to you. 5 When you sound the advance, the camps that lie on the east side shall then begin their journey. 6 When you sound the advance the second time, then the camps that lie on the south side shall begin their journey; they shall sound the call for them to begin their journeys. 7 And when the assembly is to be gathered together, you shall blow, but not sound the advance. 8 The sons of Aaron, the priests, shall blow the trumpets; and these shall be to you as an ordinance forever throughout your generations.

9 "When you go to war in your land against the enemy who oppresses you, then you shall sound an alarm with the trumpets, and you will be remembered before the LORD your God, and you will be saved from your enemies. 10 Also in the day of your gladness, in your appointed feasts, and at the beginning of your months, you shall blow the trumpets over your burnt offerings and over the sacrifices of your peace offerings; and they shall be a memorial for you before your God: I am the LORD your God."

These are trumpets fashioned out of one piece of silver. A man and a woman who have been called by God for ministry are just like those trumpets. Each one has been hammered out and intricately fashioned from this one piece of silver. As we look at this silver, we need to recognize some things about silver. This might help you understand the process that you either have been in or are in currently. When silver is mined, the miners must go very deep into the earth. Once silver is brought to the surface, the silver is not pure; it is mixed with other properties, sometimes other ores. Silver is tempered in a very hot fire. When it reaches the proper temperature, certain impurities rise to the surface and the silversmith skims them off. The silver is only ready for fashioning after the impurities have been removed. Silver is very versatile. Silver reflects light, conducts heat and electricity, and kills bacteria. Silver has a pure acoustic resonance and silver captures images. Silver is traditionally used in tableware and has been used in cherished heirlooms and gifts for centuries. When a miner digs for silver, there are dirt and impurities on the silver that, to an untrained eye, might cause you to think that it is of little or no value. When God first chose us, we were just like that. Perhaps we were rough and dirty in our old life but Jesus saw potential in us and we were chosen with purpose.

I am reminded of a young girl that was pretty wild as a very young child. She grew up on the streets. She had a foul mouth and would fight even the roughest boys in the neighborhood. The girls and the boys were scared to get on her bad side. She had a family life that was violent and the things that she saw and heard made her feel like the things she did were okay. It was called "survival" In the streets that motto is, "do unto others before they do unto you." This was the silver in the earth. People would look at this child and write her off as a no good person who would never amount to anything worthwhile. She was judged before she really had a chance. However, one day Jesus came into her life and the difference He made was astounding. Someone took the time to share the love of Jesus with this young girl. She was brought to a loving church where she was taught the Word of God. That Word began to form and fashion her into the image of God. After some time, this young lady received the call of God to preach the Word of God. This is a classic example of the silver being taken from the earth and fashioned into a beautiful usable piece for God. The many tests and fiery trails that you may have endured have been to purify the silver and prepare you for the work God has chosen you to perform.

God told Moses to take one piece of silver and make two trumpets. These two trumpets can symbolize a husband and wife ministry team. Both of them are silver, and therefore each of them is intrinsically valuable.

In the Bible, silver represents redemption. Therefore, these trumpets have been redeemed. However just being redeemed is not enough. That is why wholeness and healing is a must for each member of this unique couple. Wholeness will allow the silver to be used in ways which brokenness will not.

The truth of the matter is that many people try to find a person to help make them complete and that is not why a spouse is sent to you. You are complete in Him (Jesus Christ). This is why couples with deep issues need to come before the Lord and expose their lives to a godly person in order to begin the healing process. The impurities must be purged through the Word of God, prayers and Godly counsel. The brokenness must be repaired. If the healing does not come before the marriage, you will find that sooner or later, the brokenness will surface and cause major problems in a marriage. This can, and will happen unless we go to the Great Physician our Father and make our request for healing known to Him.

The healing may take place in a counseling session with a Christian counselor or it may take the form of inner healing during worship. It can even take place in your quiet place before the Almighty God. It doesn't matter where it takes place. Just remember, be honest with yourself. Take a long hard look at yourself. Be diligent in identifying the things in you that are not contributing to becoming usable silver.

For me, those things that I have wrestled with are the tendency to be a people pleaser and being intimidated. These have hindered me for years. People who I thought were better than me would intimidate me. I would judge myself to be less than many, therefore I would not go forward in the things that I knew I could do. I would always question myself.

This purifying process may take some time and will require exposure of old unattended wounds that were hastily bandaged over, but never properly cleansed and healed.

It's like two children getting into a fight. The parents come and demand that the children apologize and they say, "sorry" to appease the adult but hurt and anger are still there. The first chance they get; they are right back at the quarrel. Why is that? It is because they did not get the matter settled to their satisfaction. Before you can be usable silver, your past must be properly healed. Make sure your wounds have been cleansed and stitched and that you take time to fully recover.

Psalms 6:2 Have mercy on me, O LORD, for I am weak; LORD, heal me, for my bones are troubled.

This procedure does not have to take a long time. It all depends on you. It depends upon your full disclosure. You cannot merely open one door of your heart. You must be willing to cry, "I surrender all." As you fully surrender to Christ, He will heal you. *"For I am the LORD who heals you." Exodus 15:26*

Silver that has been purified is then ready for service. The Lord chooses the trumpets. The choice of your spouse must be God's choice. You must submit to God's superior wisdom when waiting on your mate. You must abandon any notion of selection based solely on emotional or aesthetic considerations. You must understand that what you will, or will not become is connected to the one you marry. So, the idea of choosing your own mate should not be a consideration. *"The Lord shall choose for me." Isaiah 30:21.*

I can remember when I first laid my eyes on Michael, my first impression was that he was not my type; I had a certain kind of man in mind for me and he was not it. I thought I should marry someone who had the same interest as myself. Michael and I are very different in many ways. He was soft-spoken and somewhat shy, and I was used to young men who were the life of the party. Some people tell you to make a list and pray and ask God for a person to match the list. I have done that myself, but I have learned that there is a flaw in that kind of selection process. The problem with that is that many times we make a list out of our own fleshly desires and that is not the way Jesus chooses people. He looks at the heart. God knows exactly who we need to help us fulfill His plan and purpose.

Our choice is frequently based on outward appearances (does he /she look good?) and personality (are they nice and humorous?), family background (who are they related to?) and mutual friends (we were introduced to each other by some friends and they think that we would be a good match). Financial security (do they have money or the potential to get money like an inheritance?). None of those things alone guarantee that a person is the one God has chosen. Don't forget that man looks on the outward appearance but God looks on the heart. We evaluate people from the outside in. He chooses people from the inside out. We cannot know someone's heart. Only God knows that. Remember the selection of King David- he was chosen as the last son of Jesse. But God said this about David; *He is a man after my own heart. Isaiah 42:16b* We cannot know what someone will become; only God can see into the future. Being in Christ should result in our trusting God to bring into our life the one He has chosen for us.

Remember, silver still needs to go through an additional process-the process of being fashioned into a trumpet. This procedure involves a series of hammering, chiseling, forming, molding, buffing and polishing. In order to produce two trumpets, there must be first a cutting and then a hammering. Some rather caustic things must happen to the silver even after it has already undergone extensive procedures to make it fit for fashioning. Perhaps you've seen enough hard times and really don't care to go through anymore; but the Master has need of you! You have been chosen. What an honor. To be picked for the Master's use. Some people do not realize that being chosen is an honor. To have Almighty God look at all of His silver pieces and chose one for His eternal purpose in ministry is truly special.

The choosing will not get you on the shelf, in a beautiful cabinet, or in a velvet case. The first place you go after you have been chosen is on the anvil to separate this silver into two perfectly formed silver trumpets. The purpose of theses trumpets is to perform specific functions. If you will remember, both trumpets came from a single piece of silver. They had equal value and equal utility. The difference between the two is not intrinsic value or worth; it is operation or function. It is how they are going to be utilized in the congregation or ministry.

Many couples in ministry suffer from the misconception that one partner is more valuable than the other. Therefore, one gets more attention, and perhaps more encouragement. But if we look at how God describes these two trumpets, it is evident that value and worth are identical. The things that distinguishes them is their function.

In the Word of God, these trumpets were used to sound two different sounds. One trumpet was made to call the people together for an assembly of the congregation. It was also used for breaking camp, and for the reading of the Word. The other trumpet was used for gathering Israel together to make war, or for other military reasons, and also for rendering judgment regarding religious issues.

When these silver trumpets were blown, the people gathered with a specific purpose in mind. Depending on the sound, they knew to be joyful, to sing, or to call to remember God's providential care. The sound of the other trumpet caused the people to gird their armor, prepare their minds for instructions, for marching orders, or for an understanding of the political situation around about them.

These two trumpets were of equal importance for the congregation to prepare them for any given situation. Each of them had their own unique role to play in the day-to-day life of the congregation. The sound of each trumpet was important to the peace and harmony of the congregation. This is where many clergy couples miss their calling and purpose. Each trumpet must be respected and honored. Each unique sound must be carefully heeded. Well-meaning parishioners who do not understand this principle will try to make you "sound" a different sound; one that you were not fashioned for; one that will cause confusion in the congregation. What if you were asked to play a lullaby for a baby with a set of cymbals? That would bring very undesirable results. This is what happens when you yield to pressures of men and make sounds you are not designed or instructed of God to make.

Clergy couples need to know the sounds they are instructed by God to make and to yield to the Lord for the enhancing and developing of that sound. We all need to grow and mature and deepen our walk with God in order to improve on the sound we make in the congregation.

There was a ministering couple that shared with us one time the disheartening fact that people in their church seemed to expect both of them to have the same abilities. The husband was very talented in the area of music. He could sing and play instruments. He directed the choir both locally and nationally. She on the other hand could sing but that was not her passion.

She felt forced into choirs and the music arena just because she felt the pressure of others upon her to make the same sound her husband made. This became a very frustrating way for her to live.

The sounding of each trumpet produced various results. Don't ever gauge yourself by other couples in ministry as to the sound each partner should make. Lay before the Lord yourselves and wait for Him to give you your own special notes. Then respect each other's "song."

As I look back over my life and think about the route that the Lord has taken me, I can't help but appreciate the complex process that I have gone through. I have become more and more aware that my life is constantly in the hands of the Lord. He has orchestrated my life from the beginning. My experiences are different from my husband's and many times early in our marriage, I did not understand the sounds he made in certain situations. I can now see that the things that God had taken me through and the things that my husband had been through were for the developing of our uniquely different characters. We were each birthed with purpose and destiny within the greater plan of God.

Early in our lives, the ministry was not in our

thoughts. Michael was immersed in his studies and was bent on becoming a dentist and making his family proud of him. He had goals in life, which did not always recognize the Lordship of Jesus Christ. I had a different point of reference. I can remember early in life wanting to work in the church. Singing was something that I really enjoyed and so I could see myself singing in the choir and working in other aspects of church ministry. That was the way I was brought up. My mother was a church worker and she instilled that in my brothers and me and that was just the way it was. As a child, I was taught to work in the house of the Lord. You didn't need a special calling to clean the church, or wash dishes or sweep the floors or replenish the toilet paper in the women's restroom. Working in God's house was a love that developed through the years. I just loved the church and God's people. I can remember my parents giving up their bedroom for preachers to come and stay with us. My father at that time was not even a believer but he was always kindly disposed toward the people of God. I know that he was blessed for those acts of kindness. I can remember viewing preachers as larger than life characters in my young impressionable mind. The thought never crossed my mind that someday I would be married to one of God's special spokesmen.

I also failed to appreciate the significance of singing unto the Lord. Actually that was a command in the Word of God. *"O Sing unto the Lord..." Psalms 96:1.* Singing unto the Lord is worship and the Lord is seeking those who will worship Him in spirit and in truth. Just because that was in me for as long as I can recall I did not really value the songs unto the Lord, until God allowed me to realize that the songs were sung unto the Lord. Therefore, we can and must sing unto the Lord wherever we might be, whether we are at church or in our garage. Sing unto the Lord! There were times in our church when we had "annual" meetings. People came from near and far to worship with us. Our church was very friendly and they would prepare dinner for everyone who wanted to eat each day of the convention, this lasted for a week. I would help in the dining room with my mother when I got home from school. We did homework in between filling salad bowls and setting the table and many other sundry tasks that we were given. After working down in the dining room at dinnertime, we would go upstairs for the evening service. We experienced some of the most wonderful teaching and preaching, second to none in the church. What was instilled in my heart was a love for the saints of God and the desire to serve them. The only pay that we would receive was an ice cream cone at the end of the week and a pat on the head. But I loved it; and, would be very upset if I could not attend every day. Training began then, and continued on as the years progressed.

As I felt the Lord leading me to attend our organization's Bible College, I was not feeling any special call to ministry. As a matter of fact, I would actually question my being at the college from time to time because many of the students there were called by God to do specific work, and I did not have that call on my life; or so I thought.

The fashioning of the trumpets had begun. My husband was being fashioned was well. When God brought us together, we were silver but the shaping of our ministry was yet to come.

We have over time learned to appreciate and respect each other's sound. Our sounds have matured and developed. We are definitely not the exact same trumpets we were in Columbus, Ohio in 1970, when we were first united in marriage.

Throughout the rest of this book, I will refer to ministerial couples as "Silver Trumpets"

2

What Do I Bring To This Marriage?

VISION

And it shall come to pass in the last days saith God. I will poor out of my spirit upon all flesh; and your sons and your daughters shall prophesy, and young men shall see visions...Acts 2:17.

Your sons and daughters shall prophesy. Do you know that you must prophesy into the marriage? You must speak those things that are not as though they are. It is crucial that each member of the team prophesy. Make sure that prophesy is in line with the things of God. For instance, the wife may prophesy that she see them going all over the world in ministry while the husband might see them working in the vineyard right around the corner and no further. They must get in sync with the Holy Spirit and hear what "thus says the Lord." He will not tell one something, which is directly opposite of what He tells the other. These trumpets are fashioned from one piece of silver. There should not be two separate agendas in the same house. A house divided against itself cannot stand.

There might be unique assignments given to each of the partners, but this will not hinder or diminish the vision as a whole. The couple will still be used mightily of the Lord if they will seek the Lord for the vision of this marriage together.

I believe that the man receives the vision for the home. By that, I mean the big picture, or the far-reaching goals that a family must aim for. Then the wife may receive the "how to" of the vision. Somehow they must work together so that God will be glorified. Remember the Word of God. Without a vision the people perish. Without a vision a marriage will perish. See the family growing in faith and love. See yourself out of debt. See yourself having enough to give to the

Kingdom. See yourself doing a mighty work for the Lord. See yourself and your family living in the perfect will of God, whatever that might be. See yourself overcoming and developing in strength and power. See yourself walking in total submission to Christ. See your children growing, learning and developing into fine godly people. See your ministry as a breeding ground for the seed of the word of God to germinate, grow and blossom into a fully mature tree of righteousness. See yourselves strengthening the body of Christ and winning souls through many means.

What do you see through the Spirit of the Lord? Don't be afraid to ask God for the vision that you need for your marriage. After He shares the vision with you, share it with your spouse. Write down the vision and make it plain that he/she who hears it may run. Not run away from the vision, but run with it. The spouse cannot run with you if you have not shared the vision with him/her. As a man of God, you may not get the whole vision all at once, but be sure to share the unfolding vision with your spouse as you receive updates. Communication is very import. Don't be afraid to speak what the Lord has shown you and don't be intimidated if you feel like you only have a little bit now. Just keep the channels of communication open to relay the latest information.

You may find that your wife is not opposed to the vision at all. She, in fact, may be feeling the specifics of the visions you share. You may also find that what God is showing you will take time, prayer and much determination to come to fruition. If you are sure that God has given the vision, you will be able to conquer each and every obstacle. Also, with the vision will come the goals. Setting goals should be a joint effort, because the goals are the little steps to get the vision accomplished. Stay prayerful and lean heavily on the arm of the Lord Jesus Christ. I can't stress that too strongly. We have far too many ministries that had begun leaning on the Lord but, as the years went by, have reverted to leaning on the arm of flesh, and it will ultimately lead to failure.

Vision is very important because it will help you stay focused and will help you set the goals that are needed to fulfill your divine purpose. Keep the vision ever before you and never allow distractions to take your eyes off the goal. Remember that the vision is "yet for an appointed time" so don't get discouraged if the vision that God shows you has not unfolded in a short time. God does not measure time like we do. He knows everything and He knows the appointed time for each season of your life. He knows how many tests and how many trials it will take to get you to the place where He wants you to be. Trust the Lord!

Mike had a vision of us being actively involved in the ministry. His vision first was for us to go out on the evangelistic field and minister full time traveling from city to city. He saw himself preaching and I would sing. Upon sharing his vision with me, I began to carry that vision in my heart and I began to observe evangelists that would visit our church and I would ask them all kinds of questions. Especially the questions of how they managed to travel with their children. I did not have any children at the time but I was preparing for the fulfillment of the vision.

ENERGY

He giveth power to the faint; and to them that have no might he increaseth strength. Isaiah 40:29

As a silver trumpet, you really need energy. You need energy to battle the flesh that will talk to you and tell you why you should be like everybody else. You will need energy to battle the unclean spirits that will war against you.

Some trumpets might ask the question why can't we go home immediately after service like other people? Why do we have to wait until the last person is ready to leave? The deacon's family might ask, why do we always get call for a ride, we were planning to ride alone and just be together. Why do we have to give our last ten dollars in the offering? I have seen several people walk past the offering plate and either drop in a few coins or they just touched the plate and put nothing in. Why do our children get more criticism than other children or why can't they make a mistake without it becoming a major catastrophe? Why aren't we allowed to have a bad hair day or just a bad day? Why are our weaknesses so vividly pointed out? Why do we seem to be the topic of conversation around the church? Why? Why? Why?

You need energy to overcome these kinds of questions and attacks. You need energy to pray and fast for yourself and others, you need energy to walk into the house of God and be a vessel unto honor. You need energy to love people who you suspect do not care if you lived or died. You need energy to love those who hate you and those who say all kinds of evil against you.

You will need supernatural energy. The energy that I speak of is not something that comes from taking vitamins, or exercising or any other natural source. This energy comes from the Spirit. David says it this way,

"He restoreth my soul." That means that He give me energy to go on, especially when I think I cannot make another step. *"Thy God hath commanded thy strength; strengthen, O God, that which thou has wrought for us." Psalms 68:28*

You will need energy to raise your family and train them in the way they should go. Spend time with your family. You will need energy to be consistent with discipline and compliments. I am not just talking about all being in the same car traveling to and from services or church. I am not talking about all being in the same house but everyone is in a different room with different agendas. When your family is young they need both the trumpets sounded in the home. Schedule a time when the family gets together for fun and relaxation time together.

When our children were young we set aside one evening when we called it family night. This was a night when we devoted all our attention to them. We talked and laughed, we had pillow fights and we played games. Our children came to look forward to those evenings. I can say that the people in our church would respect that night also. I read a book some years ago entitled **Making a Memory** authored by Mrs. James Dobson and Mrs. Gloria Gaither. In that book, these women shared things that would help you create good memories for the family so that when your children grew up they would be able to look back on their lives and remember some great times. Some of those times just happened, and sometimes you have to make them happen. You want your children to look back over their lives in a ministry household with fondness not bitterness.

My husband always tried to take the family on a vacation every summer, and places he would chose were fun and exciting. Not always expensive, because we did not always have the money to go to fancy theme parks or faraway places. Sometimes we rented a two bedroom cottage on a lake in Michigan and spent a week boating and fishing and cooking over an open fire, making each other laugh and telling stories. We roasted marshmallows and made s'mores. In the evening we would sit around the fire and talk until some of the children would fall asleep. We would take them to bed and return to the camp fire and just reflect. Those were great times with little money. It just required planning and desire. To this day our children remember those times with fondness. Our son recalls the time he and his dad went fishing in a small boat and they caught a fairly large catfish and the catfish was screaming in the boat and Steve, our son, decided to hit the catfish with one of the oars. This brought great fear due to the possibility of capsizing the boat. When they returned to the shore they talked about this fish experience and we all laughed and had a great time. They made a memory.

Many times, couples in ministry are working so hard to "grow" in a ministry that they neglect their own family. They only respond to crises and trouble. There have been well known ministers who, after years of ministering all over the world, have said, "I have preached, taught, and prayed for many people. Everyone knows my name, but my children don't know me and my wife and I have drifted apart." This is a sad commentary for silver trumpets.

To keep a balance, it will take energy and planning. It will require energy to deal with situations and not ignore things until they become critical. Many people would rather take an "ostrich head in the sand" approach. Or they believe no news is good news, or "please don't tell me anything and then I won't be responsible for it." None of the above is pleasing to God nor will they improve your marriage or your family. Instead they will hinder your "sound" in the ministry.

You will need energy to work on yourself. Don't look in the mirror of God's word and forget what manner of person you are. As you look in the mirror and see areas that need work, you will need energy to change them. You will need energy to rid yourself of bad habits and to develop good habits.

You will need to bring to the "silver trumpet connection"- energy to live a life that brings glory to God. The energy required enables you to take direct hits and eventually get back up again.

Once there was a couple that was very active in the ministry. They themselves were not pastoring, however they worked very closely with the pastor. They were high profiled in their church. They were moving along well, working diligently and they felt their relationship with the pastor and other leaders in the church were good. One day a situation arose in the church concerning the wife. She was the choir director and she was accused of maligning one of the pastor's children. This was not true but it was a gross misunderstanding. The wife was not given an opportunity to share or explain what really happened. The issue got worse when the pastor rebuked her openly in front of many members of the congregation. She was devastated and visibly wounded. Her husband saw the tears in her eyes and questioned what happened. After relaying all the gory details the husband began to feel the pain of his wife. They both were hurt deeply. Listen, church hurt is real, but remember it is not likely that the whole church hurts you, it is actually a person or persons in the church. They went out of town for a few days. During that time they thought of many things. "We should leave this church; they don't respect us or love us. We should go somewhere that the love of Jesus Christ is evident." They cried and talked. They were hurting. "Why didn't the pastor ask for both sides? Why didn't the pastor see right through this? Doesn't he know us; doesn't he know that we would never do such a thing? Maybe we should go back and talk to them and explain what really happened?" "No, that would not work, because they really don't want to hear it, if they had wanted to hear it they would have asked before it got to such an elevated level." At this point the couple is operating in the flesh. That will get you nowhere. You can wallow in self-pity, which will lead to bitterness, or you can forgive. The evidence of true forgiveness is that they could remember and re-tell the event with no pain and no bitterness. They asked God for help, and he did help them. This couple made the decision to forgive and continued to work for the Lord. This came after much prayer and fasting and seeking the Lord. This is an example of silver trumpets getting up after a direct hit. Satan meant it for evil, but God meant it for good!

Silver trumpets call upon the energy God has given you to rise. You must get up for your sake, your spouse's sake, your family's sake, and the ministry's sake. God will give you energy to rise again. After a severe test, you may not bounce back the very next day, but energy God has and will provide you will bring you back. After a direct hit, you will come back stronger, and wiser. If we don't learn from each test, then what purpose did they serve?

I bring the energy to seek God for the wisdom and knowledge that I must glean from every situation.

STABILITY

For I know the thoughts that I think toward you, saith the Lord, thoughts of peace, and not of evil, to give you an expected end. Jeremiah 29:11

Stability is steadiness, or firmness of purpose. This is crucial in a ministry marriage because there is always something trying to shake you. Something to unsettle you and cause you to doubt yourself, doubt your spouse, doubt the voice of God in your life, doubt your purpose, doubt the vision. If you can bring stability to the marriage, it will cause the whole family to feel safe and secure. It is no wonder that one of the key assaults to any marriage is instability.

In our frailties as human beings we allow doubt to creep into our minds from time to time. This usually happens when something goes wrong or we are not seeing things happen the way we thought they should. Let's say a pair of silver trumpets has felt the leading of the Lord to begin an evangelistic outreach in a particular neighborhood. They have a great vision of the many people who would come and be fed and clothed and receive the gospel. They do all the homework necessary for such an endeavor; they speak with their pastor and get the backing of the church membership, both financially and physically. They begin with tremendous support from their local church and they are very encouraged. As they continue, lives are changed for the Kingdom of God. They have many to assist them and things are great. Over time, the church goes through a financial difficulty and can no longer assist, but that does not deter them as they still believe that the work is worthwhile. They begin supporting the outreach from their own personal finances. Then the helpers began to diminish which left the two of them carrying the load. This begins to weigh heavily on them and their marriage. They begin to doubt the voice of the Lord that they heard some months back.

Most of our doubt usually stems from some conflict or adversarial situation we have encountered. Just because you have run into some hard times does not mean you did not hear God's voice speaking to you. Many times it means that you did hear God's voice and you are being buffeted to distract or derail you from the work you have been called to do.

You may have to re-visit your vision. You may spend time in prayer, but you cannot lose your stability. One way to remain steady is to stand on God's Word. When things are hurled at you, get the Word of God, read what He says about the situation you are facing and stand on His Word.

Your prayer should be something like this: "God you said _____ and I am standing on what you said. I'm not giving up and I am not giving in. I'm not throwing in the towel." You may have to say it over and over until it connects in your spirit. Stability is essential in your marriage.

If you don't possess stability, ask God for it. I'm not talking about changing your mind about the color of the walls or about what you like to eat. You have that privilege. I'm talking about the permanence of your marriage and the ministry. When things don't turn out just right, you are not looking for an opportunity to bail out. Stability says that you are in it for the long haul.

COMPANIONSHIP

I am a companion of all them that fear thee, and of them that keep thy precepts. Psalms 119:63

Two Silver Trumpets

There is a song that says, *"Lean on me when you're not strong, I'll be your friend, I'll help you carry on, for it won't be long when I'm going to need somebody to lean on...we all need somebody to lean on..."* That's what silver trumpets should bring to the marriage – a comrade kind of attitude. I'll be the one you can look to for an encouraging word. I'll be your comrade in battle. A definition of companion is, "one of a pair or set." A true companion is one with whom I share my innermost feelings; my friend and confidant. There should be such a fellowship between the two trumpets that, over time, you will be able to interpret each other's facial expressions and body language across a crowded room.

Companionship means the two of you lean on each other. I don't heap all the work on you; we share the load. I can feel when you are tired and need a break from the routine. Or I understand your need to be alone and I will respect that, but won't be far away. Just breathe a sigh of relief. Why? - because you are my comrade.

In ministry, we are engaged in a real spiritual war. The war is between evil spirits and the children of God. Therefore, you need a comrade in battle, someone who has "got your back" – not **stabbing** you in the back!

Michael and I have a kind of camaraderie that I believe has developed over time. The beautiful thing about silver trumpets is the fact that they are always in the hands of the master craftsman. You must realize that undermining each other hurts both people. I have the utmost confidence in God, that He is carefully and strategically bringing us to a desired end. I am just human, Michael is just human and we might fail each other even if we don't mean to, but God will help our infirmities.

Fighting each other is like shooting yourself. I refuse to allow other's comments about my husband to affect the way I love him or treat him. In the toughest battles, when it might be easier on me to remain silent, I cannot let him go into battle and face the enemy without the knowledge that I will be right beside him. I know the same goes for him concerning me. I am not saying go along with each other in wrongdoing. There is a time and place to correct or make right, but not in public. Make the corrective statements in private. If you try to correct in public you will get a negative reaction because you have embarrassed them. They might receive your correction if it is done in private and done in love.

What can make a ministry marriage strong are the things you go through together. Michael and I have been through many things and the one thing I can truly say is that we both derive strength from each other. I remember a time when our home caught fire. During the event we operated as one, never once did we feel like we did not trust the other one. There was a total and complete trust. He demonstrated a primary concern for me and the children and our safety at the risk of his own safety and health. He saw to it that we were out of the house safely, and then he returned to a burning house to try to put the fire out. That is a comrade!

We have been through family deaths and births of children, illness and miraculous healing, disappointments and surprise blessings, job promotions and financial difficulties. We have survived hurts and pain, joys and victories, and we can honestly say that through the many events, both good and bad, it has strengthened us as silver trumpets. To offer someone companionship is to offer them your support and loyalty through thick and thin.

RESOURCES

But my God shall supply all your need according to his riches in glory by Christ Jesus. Philippians 4:19

Resources can be described in many ways and take many forms. They may consist of material wealth, talents, resourcefulness or anything that is ready for immediate use or can be readily drawn upon for aid. Think about what kind of resources you have to contribute. Many people view only wealth or material assets as viable resources necessary for a healthy marriage and a strong ministry, however, I believe that the gifts and talents that God has given you, if you put them to good use, will be just as valuable as material wealth.

Finances are necessary because we need them to negotiate in the world. You need to know the "sound" you both make in the area of finances. Usually one trumpet is better at budgeting, planning and spending. Set goals for the family and support each other in this area. Know that God will bless and help if you put Him first. Pay your tithes. That is a must if you desire to have God open the windows of heaven. Live within your means. It causes a tremendous amount of stress on a marriage when money is a problem. Many couples have money issues from time to time. That's not what I'm referring to. I'm talking about a habitual financial struggle. This problem may require intervention from a reliable Christian financial counselor. Swallow your pride and ask for help. There is no shame in asking for help. The shame would be if you needed help and didn't ask for it because you don't want anyone to know you are in need. This becomes a matter of pride, which you can ill-afford to entertain.

Pride is not a terrible word. We need a certain amount of pride to keep things neat and clean and in order in our lives. But when pride rises to a level that prevents you from getting help- that is dangerous. That kind of pride can kill your sound as a trumpet. I do not mean that you must tell everyone what is going on, but find someone you have confidence in and who has the ability to assist you in money management. Ask for their help. Be prepared to make some changes. You cannot continue down the same road. It has been said that insanity is to keep doing what you have always done and expect a different result. There may have to be major changes to turn things around. Just know that help is not far away. Just ask! Your sound will be greatly improved.

Both trumpets need to mutually understand what it will take to operate a household. With this understanding, you can then pull in the same direction. You won't find one making an expensive purchase without consulting the other. Don't have such a tight budget that you can't buy a package of gum without counting the cost. This too could lead to a life of frustration. Each person should have some money of his or her own with which to do as they please. They also need to pool their resources to make the household run smoothly.

Some families have resented the ministry because much of their finances have gone into the ministry without any discussion and the family has gone lacking. I do not believe this is the plan of God. You know you can endure a lot if you understand the rationale behind things. Your family will not resent the ministry using your personal finances if you help them understand. God is a good paymaster, and we are not sacrificing for nothing. This is an investment into the kingdom of God. The Word of God tells the man to take care of his family. If he does not care for his family, he is worse than an infidel. Make sure that your motive is right and your priorities are right. Make sure you are yielded to God. *Seek first the Kingdom of God and his righteousness and all these things shall be added unto you. (Matthew 6:6)*

One time we counseled with a couple who were having financial difficulties. The husband wanted to travel around the country to preach the gospel and rely on the honorariums to support his family. He and his wife had full time jobs and without discussing the matter with his wife he quit his job and began to preach around the country. He thought that his wife's full time job and honorariums he would receive could sustain the family. The household finances were quickly depleted and the wife felt like she needed to get an additional job just to make ends meet. This arrangement was causing major problems in this marriage. The wife then began to resent the husband's ministry, perhaps her attitude would have been better if they had discussed and prayed about it and if they had come to some kind of decision together. After several months various meetings that he thought he was going to have did not materialize and they were struggling. He then thought about it and reluctantly sought part-time employment.

Money is a major problem in many marriages and when someone can equate the struggle to the lack of money and then connect that to the ministry, this can cause serious conflict and resentment.

As I previously stated, there are other resources that will benefit a marriage and ministry. Your God-given ability to organize, your ability to counsel, or listen are valuable resource. Your ability to write, sing, or aptitude with technology may be resources that will benefit the ministry and marriage. **Use what you have!**

Denise S. Millben

3

That's His Ministry

While I was growing up I was always intrigued with ministers and their spouses. I would watch and listen intently to the things they said and did. They rarely spoke to me, but I listened in on their adult conversations. I would not say a word and they frequently spoke freely in my presence because I became invisible to them. I heard many things that I did not repeat or even think much about at the time. Some of those things have surfaced in my mind years later for the sole purpose of sharing now. I actually heard minister's wives make statements like; I'm not into all of that, referring to the church or some activity that is going on. Or, I'm not opening my home and heart to anybody, these people are a mess. I'm his wife not those people's friend. Even at a young age I knew in my heart that those statements were just not right.

There are people who have been called by God to do a specific thing and, perhaps, when they received the call they were not married. Some people think that if they have been called and fail to acknowledge that call or merely ignore it for years, that God has changed His mind and has gone on to use someone else. If God has called you for a job, He hasn't changed His mind just because you have refused to obey. There are times, however, when God will call you but will not commission you to go until later. If that is the case, then that is God's business. Just make sure that you are not the hold up. God called Moses, and at first he had many excuses as to why he was a poor choice. Remember that God is sovereign and does not make mistakes.

I have heard minister's spouses say that the ministry is his or hers and, "I'm not into that." This is totally against the Word of God. "And these two shall be one flesh." This is the Word of God and the will of God. Marriage is not a sideline or hobby; neither is worship and service to God. Some people feel that if they are not as outgoing as their spouse, or as "anointed", or as committed, or as in love with the ministry, they mistakenly make the proclamation; they are not a part of their spouse's ministry. That is a lie! The fact remains that you are the companion trumpet and you are not required to be exactly like your spouse. You have been called to blow a "complementary" sound.

Pastors, who have wives or husbands that are not involved in the ministry, in some way, need to earnestly seek the Lord for His will to be revealed to your spouse. The ministry of the 21st century requires that both trumpets operate at capacity. It is much easier for people to lay claim to a personal ministry so that they do not have to be involved in the church because I have my own ministry. No one knows what it is but they claim to have one, this way they can escape spiritual accountability, and that is vital to the work of the Lord. Some people are just plain lazy. Sometimes there are other things that enter into the picture and hinder the operation of the second trumpet. Sometimes it is fear and intimidation. Fear that they will be compared to their spouse and fail to measure up to their potential. There is no need to be fearful. You are the other trumpet; you have been fashioned by God for His purpose. Please don't minimize the assignment you have been given by the Lord. Above all, do not compare yourself with any other person-not even your spouse. You are unique in your call and in your purpose. It is very important that you be fully persuaded of the will of God.

I spoke to a minister's wife, she was disconnected from her husband's ministry. She came to church but left immediately after the service, and has little or no communication with the membership. Her complaint was that the people don't respond to her. She felt like the congregation wanted her to sing, and since she couldn't sing or play an instrument, she felt like she had no function. She felt isolated, ignored, and unwanted. I began to ask her what were her strong interests, or what did she enjoy doing? After some conversing, she discovered that decorating was something she was good at and enjoyed. She now uses her talents to beautify the house of the Lord. She now feels connected to the membership and the ministry because she has something to contribute. She found out the sound she was supposed to make.

It might take some time to discover it, but everyone is good at something, so find out what that something is and do it with all your might. Each trumpet has a sound that must be sounded in order to have a complete and accurate work of God.

Often spouses may have a faulty concept of ministry. By definition, ministry is serving and working to act as one's agent. You may not realize that the gracious words you speak, the comforting gestures, the encouraging way you answer the phone, or even the way you keep the home organized and operating smoothly, is ministry.

To be a person of integrity and honor is a sound that must be heard clearly in the ministry. There will be an attempt by the adversary to stop and block the blowing of the two trumpets. That is why you may be having tension in your home as well as in your spirit. You may even begin to loathe the ministry. The perception is that if we were not in the ministry we would have a _____you fill in the blank. But the real truth is that being involved in the ministry is not a burden if everyone is carrying part of the load. Take a look at yourself and your attitude. Check out why you have this attitude. Have you allowed the enemy to plant some seeds in your heart that will destroy your ministry and destroy you if you continue in this vein?

Every now and then you need to ask God to do a heart check for you. Lord if you find anything that is not pleasing to you, take it out. Any seed that was not planted by the Lord must be uprooted. Do you remember the story in the Bible about a field that had weeds in it? The servant asked the master if the seed was bad. The Master replied no, the seed is okay but an enemy has sown weeds among the good seed. When you ask God to do a heart check He will show you the things that the enemy has sown in your heart. When you see it get rid of it as quickly as possible.

Let's take a look at what you are. Just for a minute, look at you. Who are you? Why are you the way you are? Who has added to, or taken from your perfect design to create the person that stands before you in the mirror? The way you are right now is the sum total of all your life experiences. All of your experiences combined have created this person. Is this who you really want to be or is there another person longing to emerge? The combination of stressful events, hostile environments and broken relationships-all conspire to undermine and distract the birthing of the true you God has in mind. We are not our own; but we have had many life experiences, some bad, and some absolutely terrible. All these things have impacted our lives to such a degree that they have played a great part in making us who we are. These things have been introduced into our lives for us to grapple with and preserve. Unfortunately, some have allowed these events in life to embitter them and make them spiteful. The Bible refers to it as a "root of bitterness."

The Bible does not infer that there is not cause for the bitterness. Many of the stories that people have shared down through the years indicate legitimate reasons for bitterness, but God clearly cautions us to be on guard against that very thing. This prompts me to conclude that we are vulnerable to this condition, but need not succumb to it.

Often many people have the knowledge of how to prevent a root of bitterness from springing up in their lives. There are many that feel justified in allowing bitterness to engulf them. It may even feel good for a time to wallow in the hurt and the pain, or to make excuses for the constant rehearsing and nursing of wounds that have been inflected by others. But eventually that root will grow into a ridged, unyielding, cold wall of distrust. In Christ, you can actually uproot the tree and tear down the wall and wholly trust God with your lives. There are many that have not actually trusted God with their total lives. Therefore, when entering into the ministry, we often come hurting and undelivered and we try to blow a certain sound but what comes out sounds all wrong. This is because it is wrong! First let's get this trumpet sanctified, which means "set aside." The deliverance that is needed must take place in order for the true sound of this silver trumpet to come through. Give yourself wholly, to become holy!

In Christ you can actually start over. "Forgetting those things which are behind," and "reaching forward to those things ahead." Can we get amnesia and forget all the things in the past? No, but we must choose to release those painful, hurtful, devastating, things in our past. They have the ability to change us into a person even we don't like. You have a choice! Forget those things. You can choose to hold on to those things but realize they are like venomous snakes biting and re-biting you, filling you with poison that will leave you hurting, unfulfilled and impoverished and hurting others. Did you know that hurting people hurt people? Or you can choose to release every one of the hurts, and pick up the peace and healing that God offers.

You won't forget the events, but the pain and bitterness associated with them will be gone. You will then be able to blow the trumpet, and the sound you will make will be liberating to others. Your sound will be that of triumphant victory. People desperately need that sound from the house of the Lord.

Two Silver Trumpets

4

His Friends, My Friends, Our Friends

Early in the lives of trumpets, there are so many issues that must be worked out and dealt with. The friends of the trumpets must be mutually acceptable to each spouse. There can be problems if one of the friends is either mistrusted or not regarded as a person with whom you can let "down your hair." All ministering couples need at least one couple that is either in ministry themselves, or understands the special needs of a ministering couple. You need someone with whom you can truly be yourself, without worrying whether you will be misunderstood. Many couples have not developed such a relationship with another couple and therefore find they are holding in a lot of things that should be released in a godly and loving atmosphere of total acceptance. You need the kind of friends that will even tell you when your ideas are not in harmony with the Word of God or with the destiny of your ministry.

It has been my observation that many couples in ministry have several acquaintances. They share stories with the evangelists that come to preach. They also share with other ministers at conferences. But their truly deep and innermost feelings and the many situations, with which they must deal daily, are not brought for in-depth discussion and prayer.

There are reasons for this closed and guarded life. There are people who really don't have your wellbeing in mind. Many couples have been "bitten" by that so-called "caring person" who invites you to "bare all." But when this unsuspecting couple, in desperate need of a listening ear, a compassionate heart and godly counsel, bares all, they encounter a person who has a hidden agenda. The baring of their souls is used as a weapon against them. If that hasn't happened to you, you have heard about it happening to someone else and it frightens you and makes you apprehensive about drawing someone close to you. I am not suggesting that you "open up" to just anyone but I do believe that God will put people in your path that can provide you with the companionship and comfort which you both will need.

Take a moment and thank God for such a person in your life, or ask God to send you someone you can share with and confide in and know that what you say will not be spoken to anyone. We must create a safe environment for people to unload.

Men need confidants as well as women. Women seem to find someone easier than men. Therefore, it is difficult to find a couple with whom both parties feel equally comfortable. The ideal case is another ministering couple. If that is not readily available, allow your spouse to share with trusted godly friends. He or she needs that outlet. As a couple, you will find that people are drawn to you for various reasons. Unfortunately, these reasons are not always above board and in line with the agenda of a true child of God. There are women who will try to get close to the wife for the sole purpose of getting close to the husband. Beware! We must stay close to God and be forewarned; and He will alert us, and will not leave us ignorant of the devices of Satan.

One time early in our marriage my husband was working full time in a secular job and ministering part time. He had quite a high-powered job. He was a personnel manager for a trucking firm. He had a private secretary. She was very good at her job; however she had some personal family problems. My husband was someone that she could talk to. She also had a spiritual need and, since he was a minister, it only seemed logical for her to speak to him about her problems. These conversations began to continue even after he would get home from work. Before he could get in the door sometimes, she would call and talk about the family business. I was feeling so sorry for her and her dilemma. This went on for a while; it did not upset me because she had such a need. I really thought my husband was making headway that was leading to her coming to Christ. I must admit sometimes I would not like the fact that she would call during dinner and he would talk until the meal was cold.

One day she called and he had not come in from work yet and I asked if I could help. There was some hesitancy, but she began to tell me what was going on at that time. As I listened I began to pray for her because it was serious. I could see that it was going to take more time than I had at the moment, so I told her that I was going to be leaving in a short time but I would be back later in the evening. I invited her over to our home when I returned. She said that would be fine. I let my husband know what had taken place and he was comfortable with that. While I was gone, she came over knowing full well that I was not there. She was desperate to talk to someone and this put my husband in a precarious situation.

When I returned home, my husband told me that she had come while I was away. He talked to her briefly, but he felt awkward with her there and cut the conversation short and invited her to come over when I was home. Needless to say I was furious. This meant that she did not respect him or me because that put him in a bad situation. I expressed my feelings concerning this young lady. I also prayed and asked God to show me if I was overreacting. I was honest with my husband and told him that I thought she had her eyes on him. I ran the risk of sounding like a jealous wife. He respected my sound and we began to pray and ask God to do something to help us if she was up to no good. After all, he had to work with her every day. Shortly after we prayed, this woman went on vacation and when she returned she was offered a job with another company and she quit the job and moved. God will not leave you ignorant.

I am beginning to see clearly that the devil hates

families and especially those families who are dedicated to the work of the Lord. Ministers seem to be the prime target of the attack of the enemy. Husbands and wives need to travel together and be seen together as much as possible. This sends a statement to anyone who has immoral plans, that you are together and happily married.

Please let that be the case. I believe He gives us the sensitivity in the spirit. Listen to the sound of the Spirit! It is imperative in this time, because the ministry is under an attack. Two major areas that seem to be in the forefront of the destruction of ministries are sex and money.

Satan comes to steal, kill and destroy. He will steal your marriage, kill your ministry and ultimately destroy you and your spouse. At this point, I may sound old-fashioned, but through observation and godly wisdom, I venture to say that a close relationship between a husband and another woman, single or married is unhealthy and provides a breeding ground for unhealthy conversation, and fertile soil for Satan to sow seeds of unfaithfulness in hearts that were formerly innocent and upright. If nothing else, it can leave room for your good to be spoken of as evil. This, in the long run, can damage your ministry.

In ministry we must remember we are not our own, but we have been bought with a price. God is our Master and Guide. As two silver trumpets, we must learn to trust each other's gifts and be sensitive to each other. If your spouse remarks, "I don't have a good feeling about this or that," recognize that God may be allowing them to see or sense something that you don't. The trumpet must sound a certain sound. If you both are committed to God and to each other, you will realize that neither is trying to harm the other.

In this age, there is a definite need for discernment. Trust the Spirit of God to work on your behalf. I don't care how easy a person of the opposite sex may be to talk to, ask God to send you a person of the same sex to confide in. Give no place to the devil. Make sure you are always available for your spouse. Give that understanding ear and that wise counsel. *"If any one lacks wisdom, let him ask God who gives liberally and upbraided not..." (James 1:5)*

Friends are important. The Bible refers to a friend as a support, a comfort, help, and guide. The ministering couple should seek to become each other's best friend as well as having other friends. Friends are rare and hard to find, but sorely needed. Friendship doesn't require communicating every day or even weekly. It does mean knowing when you need to get together; it is not a strain to do so. You must make time for friends, including them in times of recreation and relaxation as well as serious downloading time. Have friends with whom you can laugh.

Michael and I have been blessed with many friends. We have friends that we have traveled with, we have laughed and joked with and had great times together. We have also cried and prayed with them. This has been healthy and good for them and us. We have some good friends who are involved in ministry. We share problems and they understand because they have either faced similar situations or are currently experiencing something as well.

I now believe that God will bring people into your life not only to help you, but for you to also help them. Some friends are lifelong friends and other friends are only in your life for a season. It is important that you understand this concept. If you think that all friends are your friends for life, you can be sorely disappointed when friends drift away from you or the relation-ship is damaged. Perhaps the friendship developed when either you needed some strength from that person or they needed something from you. As a result, you both drew closer and a friendship developed. But after the issues were solved and time had healed the wounds, there was not a need for that friendship to be sustained, and so over time you drifted apart. Sometimes your friendships take a new turn if you are miles away from a friend. The friendship is still there, but you are not as close as you once were. This is neither good nor bad; it is just the way it is. How-ever, you must strive to maintain certain relationships because even Jesus had friends.

Two Silver Trumpets

5

The Christian Marriage

What does the Lord require from the sliver trumpets? It is my belief that the Lord does expect certain things from us as men and women of God. The example that we are to set before the world is very important. The Lord requires that our marriages reflect the relationship of Christ and His church.

In the world today, the state of matrimony is too often a "take-take" situation. But the philosophy that the saint of God should envelop is God-like thinking. As

I observe and perceive the things that are happening to the silver trumpets in the Body of Christ, my heart begins to reach out to the saints. Silver trumpets need to know that they can be married and be involved in the ministry and still have a successful and fulfilled life. I do not think that it is an either/or situation that means either you will have a beautiful marriage and a loving home life, or you will have a successful ministry. We have been married and actively involved in the ministry, and I can honestly say that I am more in love with him than I was during our times of courtship and he has said the same thing. We are experiencing a move of God in the ministry but it is not at the expense of our personal relationship or the relationship of our family. The dynamics have changed through the years but the love has not been diluted. God's Word has told us that we are to have "life" and "that more abundantly." That means that we can live and *really* live. My prayer early on in our marriage was, "Lord, teach me how to make our home a haven of rest." After you have worked in the ministry you both need to be able to come home to a safe place.

I have read many books concerning marriage, which have benefited me, but I can honestly say that there is not one book on the market that can do the work for me-this book included. You have got to want to make this marriage and the ministry successful. The Word of God says, *"Commit thy way unto God and He shall bring it to pass."*

This book is written to the husband and wife that are totally sold out to the Lord and to the plan of God. We, the ministers of the great gospel of Jesus Christ, can get so lopsided in our service to God that we can miss the blessings that God wants to heavily bestow upon each and every one of us. I have spoken to many men and women in ministry that simply do not know how to juggle the work and the life. It is a sad commentary on the clergy to say that many of our younger couples do not understand that the Lord has called them to do a work for Him. It is important that you get a clear understanding of the work you have been called to perform or you may find yourself jealous of someone else's calling and longing to be something that you are not. My best advice is to find out who **you** are in Christ first. You may not know all that God wants you to do in your lifetime, but you **can** know the direction that He wants you to go.

The first question that you must ask yourself is what do I bring to this marriage? Whole-ness in one's heart and spirit is a must for a whole marriage. If a person is splintered while single, getting married will not make him or her whole. You must be made whole before you commit to a life with another person. Take some time for self-reflection, and introspection. You must ask yourself; do I bring bitterness to this marriage? Do I bring hurts to this marriage that could surface, given the right set of circumstances? Lay every one of these hurts and unforgiven issues, and broken promises and other relationships that went sour, at the feet of Jesus Christ and surrender them. Ask Him to take each one and fill the void that this pain or hurt has created. Ask Him to fill these places with His love and joy and peace. Make sure that there is not a place in your heart that you have not opened to the Lordship of Christ.

You may need to go through a cleansing process; the washing of your heart by the Word of God. You may need to face old issues that have never been dealt with, things that you thought were dead and buried are issues that may surface when certain things occur like certain music playing or a scent that reminds you of an event from years past or brings an old issue back to mind. Your mood and your behavior suddenly changes and you don't even understand it your-self. But here you are dealing with the old hurt in the presence of a new situation. My brothers and sisters, you must be healed from these old things or they will affect the way you handle the new issues in your life. It does not have to take long, but you must get yesterday's pain out of your heart, so that it will not impact the way you deal with your today. Yesterday can enhance today and tomorrow or it can destroy them. Or at the very least, yesterday's unhealed issues can cripple today and handicap tomorrow.

In a study of anything that reflects godly Christian lives, we must use the Word of God as the guide for all the discussion. The Bible is the standard that we must use for our instruction and direction. What is the role of the husband according to the Word of God? We will have to be careful not to go to the secular world for instruction and direction on the subject. Let me make it perfectly clear that I regard the Word of God as the ultimate and final answer to the problems that face marriages today, especially the silver trumpets.

So what does the Word say the role of the Man is in this relationship we call marriage? *"Let the husband render unto the wife due benevolence." (I Corinthians 7:3)* What does this mean? The understanding that I would like to share is that the husband must relinquish the exclusive right to his body and give the wife the right to it. The husband must give freely and generously and show kindness to the wife.

Genesis 2:24 declares, *"Therefore shall a man leave his father and mother, and shall cleave unto his wife; and they two shall be one flesh."* God, in the beginning, ordained marriage and the family unit as the first and most important institution on earth. God's plan for marriage is one male and one female that become physically and spiritually united. They become "one flesh."

The world's influence upon us today is so strong that we must fight to resist its philosophy about marriage. For that reason, I have been referring to the Bible throughout this book in order to keep divine perspective and to remind us what the Lord has to say on each matter. We do not want to pollute our minds with thinking that comes from the world around us.

Also, we read in the Word of God that a man must love his wife like Christ loved the church and gave Himself for it. That is an awesome task that God has given man to perform. One thing that is wonderful to know is that the Lord does not give us a task that is a "mission impossible." The mission is possible with Jesus Christ as the head of our lives. He gives us divine order.

We will run into problems if the order is wrong. Men do not have to fight and scuffle to attain the headship in a marriage. It is God given. I'm seeing in the world today a struggle for the headship and that is not necessary, because God has already settled that in His word. The man is the head of the woman and Christ is the head of the man. If you understand the divine order, the marriage will be blessed.

What does it mean to render benevolence? The woman has been designed such that she desires to feel safe and secure. When a woman is forced into a role that is not God given, that will produce a fear that will cause her to react out of character. When the man doesn't assume his God-given role, it creates a vacuum in the relationship and even nature itself teaches that vacuums will soon be filled by something. So if a man is not fulfilling his God-ordained role, then the woman may not want to fill it, but she will do it in order to save the household. We have a Biblical account of this very thing happening. David and his men were living in a remote area and while they were out in the field they happened to encounter some servants tending the herds of a wealthy landowner whose name was Nabal. David's men watched out for the servants of Nabal and protected them from marauders. After the servant returned home, David requested Nabal to send some food to him and his men as a kind gesture for the protection of the men. Nabal heard the request and sent the messengers back with the answer, No! In his message Nabal informed David that he never asked for his protection, and was not going to help them by supplying food for them.

The servant took the message to David and it infuriated David to the point of preparing his men to go to Nabal's home and kill the people and take what they wanted.

Nabal's wife, Abigail, also heard David's request and her husband's reply. Abigail was faced with a serious dilemma. What should she do? Her husband's role is to provide and protect and cover the family, but here is a man that is not making wise choices. His decisions were put-ting the family and the household in jeopardy. Should she stand around wringing her hands and wait for David and his men to come and destroy her home and perhaps even their lives?

Abigail makes a decision to at least attempt to rescue the family. She tells the servant to load up meat, fruit, bread, and wine on several mules and she puts herself in danger to accompany the food to the camp of an angry powerful man. She now assumed the role of the intercessor. This is the role that her husband should have filled but now she is forced to fill that role for the sake of the family.

God was with Abigail and because of her stepping into another role, God softens David's heart and he accepted the food and spared the household. When Nabal heard of the heroic act of his wife, the Bible says that he got sick and died. Abigail's act was out of the proper order, but she did what she thought was best and many women have had to do this because the men would not step up to bat, so God does help and bless, but I believe that there is a price to be paid for a man not walking in his God-given position in the home. Although it might appear to be the right thing to do, down the road it could lead to disaster. I want to pause here to just say that I am speaking about women who want to be in the **perfect** will of God, the women that wants to be in God's order, which produces a place of safety, free from anxiety. A woman out of order is nervous and full of anxiety because she is forced to fulfill a role for which she was not designed to be successful. For the man, this role comes naturally, because that is his place.

God is always looking beneath what is obvious. He looks at the heart and the motive. There may be times when the trumpet cannot function for whatever reason, sickness, mental stress, etc. and the partners takes up the slack, I would like to refer to this time as a grace period, but for this to continue after the mate has recovered will wear on the relationship.

I do not mean to suggest that there are not women whose talents and abilities a wise husband should not utilize in order to help the home and ministry run smoothly. If the man sees that God has given him a wife with gifts and talents to offer the marriage in order for them to reach their maximum potential, he is wise if he asks her for her input, or seeks her counsel and encourages her to use her gifts. Love and respect is very important to any marriage and especially a marriage that is plunged into full time ministry.

The benefits are multitudinous. When trumpets are operating in their areas of gifting and calling there is peace in the home. The family walks in obedience of the silver trumpet. By ex-ample you will teach your family as well as your spiritual family what walking in divine order will bring into their lives. They will see you walking in peace, even when there is a storm about you. They will see the scripture fulfilled in you. *"I will never leave you nor forsake you." Hebrews 13:5.* **David said,** *"I was young and now I'm old and I have never seen the righteous forsaken nor his seed begging bread."*

Simply Trusting

In a marriage where both partners are involved in ministry, the trust factor must be very strong between them because there will be people and circumstances that conspire to drive a wedge between them. One of the things that each couple must focus on is not only trusting one another, but also trusting God. When we trust each other, we do not allow seeds of doubt and distrust to be dropped into our hearts as to the loyalty of our partners. On the other hand, each partner must decide and determine in his or her own heart that they will do nothing that will allow suspicion to take root in the marriage. Therefore, there are things that must be avoided at all costs.

One of those things is inappropriate contact with the opposite sex. Spending undue or inordinate amount of time with someone in counseling could be dangerous, you should always counsel someone of the opposite sex with another person nearby if the counseling takes place in your home or office, or leave the door open so that there is still a measure of privacy, but also sufficient propriety at all times. I believe that in this age there are spirits that have been assigned to destroy ministries such as the spirits of seduction. One of their main assignments is to destroy the trust factor between a husband and wife. If the husband is counseling or ministering to any woman, he needs to take special precautions to cover himself during these counseling sessions.

I have actually heard of cases where women have come to a church with the sole purpose of destroying the minister's marriage. They have come to the man with stories of pain, fear, or hurt, in order to draw the man in with sympathy. The men have an honest motive; they just want to help. They cannot see that this is a trap. Beware and cover yourself! This is not for a man to think that leadership consists of doing as he pleases with no concern for what people think, or what a situation may look like. I think that God is speaking in his ear all along the way, with warnings and nudges in the spirit. Take heed to the Spirit of God. The Bible clearly tells us to avoid or shun the very appearance of evil and we must recognize that there are men and women who have been sent by Satan to destroy our ministries and to destroy our marriages. One member of the couple must always be sensitive to what is happening and to be in a position to come against Satan's schemes with prayer and support in order to bring this victory.

If trust has been destroyed, there are ways to repair or re-build it, but it will take time, energy and effort on the part of both parties. I would like to deal first with marriages that have not suffered loss of trust. Then I will deal with marriages in with trust has been loss through lies, deceit, infidelity, etc. To the couples that have not had that trust broken, I say, count yourself blessed of the Lord! That is not something that just happens; it is a commitment on both sides. It is allowing the Lord to manage your lives. With respect to the silver trumpets, each one makes a certain sound for the congregation and the people of God, but the primary things that always ring true are trust and love. Those are strong factors in a marriage. If I trust you, this means I have put my confidence in you. We understand that God is the first and primary trust we have, but after Him we can trust one another. We must trust one another.

There are many levels of trust that God allows us to experience in life. Some of us have had difficult lives prior to our marriages, which have caused us to have a distrusting attitude. This distrust overflows into areas of our martial relationship. Example; A man has had a terrible situation in a previous marriage and he meets a wonderful woman that he believes and knows has been sent to him by God, but things that happened in the past are still hanging on and he thinks that his woman may do the same things that were done in the previous relationship therefore he puts up walls and the woman doesn't understand why the walls are up. One of the things we have to fight is bringing "old baggage" into our marriage and allowing our past to negatively influence our marriages. We need to ask the Lord to cleanse us of all that old stuff. We won't get amnesia but we definitely can stop the effects of what has happened in the past from influencing what will happen in the future. I believe the Spirit of the Lord desires us to go into our marriages and to flourish with clean slates. Nowhere, but in Christ, can you have your record wiped completely clean. Just ask the Lord to help you cancel out the effects of past hurts and injuries.

Ask the Lord to heal you from anything that would cause you to distrust your mate without a cause. As the Spirit of the Lord begins to work in your life to cause you to heal, just allow the healing to come.

One thing that cancels out distrust is an open dialog between husband and wife. They need to talk. Talk about everything even the insignificant things, even things that you think won't matter. You need to have a listening ear. It is one thing to merely hear the sounds that come from someone's mouth, but it's another thing to truly listen. This means to open one's heart and spirit to another. That is an interesting concept, to listen with your heart. If you can listen with your heart, you can begin to understand what a person is trying to say even between the lines. Sometimes people have a hard time getting to the core of what they are trying to say or what they are trying to express. This whole book is dealing with people in ministry, so hopefully and prayerfully; everyone in ministry has a level of relationship with the Lord. As you begin to listen with your heart, your spouse may be sharing some things with you that are critical. He or she may be sounding the sound that is critical not only for your marriage, but for your ministry as well.

In a marriage, God supplies all things. He gives us *"everything that pertaineth to life and godliness."* So between these two, there is a measure of the discerning of spirits, faith, mercy and grace that has been dispersed in every marriage. If you will learn to listen to each other's sound, you will reap that which God has planted in your union; a great harvest of peace, love, joy and fruitfulness in ministry. As a couple begins to recognize the sound and begins to really listen to it, they may discover that the wife is able to express some things that a listening husband may benefit from, a "sound" of warning even when she has not expressed it overtly. But if he is listening with his **heart**, there is a sound that will come forth and begin to prick his heart. His response will then be "I better take heed to this" or "I better listen", because she is saying something important. Maybe she is able to discern spirits or has a word of wisdom or knowledge concerning a particular issue. Even in casual conversation, let us learn to hear with our hearts so we're not tempted to say, "Oh, my husband is just blowing off steam" or "my wife is just nagging." Sometimes our spouses are crying out for their own personal needs to be met. "I need for someone to pay attention to me." "Give me personal attention." Maybe as adults in ministry, we feel as if we should not indulge in such self-centeredness-all of our thoughts and interests should center around our ministry to those in need. But if our personal needs are not met, it is certain that the needs of the ministry will suffer as well. There will always be a deficiency because that same deaf ear, which cannot seem to hear the needs of its companion, will also be deadened to the needs of the flock. No matter what sort of ministry you are involved in, do not ignore the sound of your mate who is laboring with you because he or she is the one who God has chosen to compliment you and to assist you in the successful fulfillment of the ministry He has called you to perform.

The two trumpets are made from one single piece of silver. Silver in the Bible always denotes redemption. This describes people who are not perfect, but who have nevertheless been re-deemed by the blood of the Lamb. You have to understand that your mate is not perfect. The only real perfection is in Christ Jesus. While maturing into the fullness of Christ, allow your mate to make mistakes and don't hold them against him or her.

My husband and I have had arguments and neither one of us wanted to admit that we were wrong, so we walked around the house not speaking and ignoring each other, when it came time for bed, how could we get on our knees and thank God for the day and ask for his blessings through the night with the weight of un-forgiveness on our shoulders? We might even press past prayer and actually get in bed and then cannot sleep, tossing and turning until finally one of us speaks in the silent darkness of the room. Are you asleep? The answer comes back slowly and softly, No! Then begins the rapid and heart-felt apologies. It may seem like you are apologizing quite frequently but that's all right. If it is necessary then by all means do it. As you determine not to let the sun go down on your wrath, then God will help you and those nights of anguish will become less and less. Move forward, mature and grow-up. Learn to hear the sound of the flesh as well as the sound of the true ministry. This will benefit your relationship tremendously. If you only listen with the ears tainted by the flesh, you won't perceive what is really being said.

It is amazing to see what happens when a couple begins to pray together (prayer set aside from personal devotions). A couple needs to pray together as a unit. This releases special sounds. If your spiritual ears are tuned to the frequency of your mate, you will begin to hear things, even in prayers that will alert you to the condition in the spirit. Our first and foremost goal should be ourselves, to draw near to God to get closer to Him; and, then our families need to be the second concern in our lives. We must be able to say, "God, I trust you to give me the wisdom I need in order to be beneficial in this union." "I trust you, to supply everything we need, to be examples of godliness in this present world." This world is full of deceit, lures and traps. There is pollution everywhere, and the very things that are in the atmosphere begin to work their way into the fabric of our homes and our lives. Lay yourself before the Lord and tell God you must trust Him to give you everything you need to be that perfect trumpet in your marriage. Trust God that He will put some things into you or that He will take some things out of you that will enable you to grow in wisdom. This process is not a one-sided thing. These two trumpets are made from the exact same piece of silver. God is working on both sides to bring us to His desired end. His desire for us is far greater than what we have ever imagined. To this end, God takes us through many tests and trials. The way we handle these situations determines whether we go forward, stand still or go backwards.

Over time, couples often develop certain signs and signals between them that can convey encouragement or signal danger. I believe God has blessed my husband and me with a marriage that came straight from heaven. But it still has required hard work. I can't say we haven't had our disagreements, arguments or other things come against us, but the bottom line is we trusted God and our marriage is committed to Him.

There have been people and circumstances sent to destroy our marriage and try to make us give up, so don't ever think that a marriage that is sent from the Lord sails along in perfect harmony at all times. There will be times of silence and even times of despair. But you must come together and communicate. Silence is not golden in a marriage. Silence undermines a relationship. You must come together and talk. Offer each other a "penny for your thoughts." Sometimes, that will take a great effort and much time. It may take a lot of pushing, especially for those who are quieter by nature. They may find it hard to share and not want to talk, but they must. This is the only way these trumpets can function successfully together.

This trust is the key to any successful relationship. There are things people hold onto in marriages that tend to pull the marriage apart. They may hold on to their children and eventually the children grow up, and move away. If they haven't developed a relationship in which they can lean on each other and believe in one another, their marriage will begin to crumble, because it has nothing upon which to stand. Even money cannot hold a marriage together. You can't hold your marriage together with love of family, good looks, or even personality. These things pass away and so will your marriage if that's all there is to it. What happens when that sparkling personality is consumed by Alzheimer's disease? There is a level of trust and love that can developed over time that will not break down even when the "bottom falls out." This kind of love and trust will empower you to endure and press on even under the most adverse conditions.

Now to those marriages in which the trust covenant has been broken. When trust has been lost through lies, deception, or infidelity, you do have a choice. You can choose to love. The Bible says love can cover a multitude of sins. That means love can enable you to look past some things, although not to the point of denial. One of the things that will rebuild trust is time. Even after true repentance has taken place and apologies made and accepted, it will still require a period of probation during which trust must be slowly reestablished. The offending party must understand that trust must be earned. If the couple desires to rebuild this marriage, it is possible through the power of Jesus Christ. If the covenant has been broken, this is not a "seal of doom" on the marriage. It can be restored.

I believe God is in the business of restoration. He can re-store the covenant, the trust, the love, and all that has been damaged. One thing that you have to be willing to say is, "God, I am willing to present to you everything that has caused this marriage to break down; everything." And you both, as a couple, just go before the Lord and you may need outside counseling. You will need deliverance because when you break a covenant, there is a spirit that begins to move and work and the trumpets become tainted. Their silver becomes tarnished and it actually affects their sound. We do not want to send uncertain sounds through tainted trumpets. This can happen when a covenant has been broken. The relationship has been compromised; it has become marred. If the husband has been unfaithful, it will affect the wife, even though she has done nothing wrong. She becomes wounded and will make an uncertain sound. It won't sound the true sound; it won't sound the sound of God because it has been battered and bruised. Abuse, lies, infidelity, create deceit, or even verbal abuse, can combine to mar the trumpet and create a sound that will cause people to arise, but arise to what?

We don't want people responding merely to our personal need or to be sympathetic to us. The whole purpose of the trumpets' sounding is to draw the body of Christ into further service, into greater love of Christ, and to call them to battle. Jesus must be the center of all we do. If we have a marred trumpet, we will begin to call people to our own need. It isn't about us; it's about Jesus. The marriage does not have to be over because a covenant has been broken, but it will require time for restoration. It will require a time of healing and it will require a time of re-polishing and resurfacing the trumpet of God so that it can sound His sound. This will take willingness on our parts. Both parties will have to say, "God, we surrender to you." The offended party must surrender his or her hurt to God. And the offender must surrender the offense to God. Both must be willing to surrender and let the healing begin and believe God for it. Believe it or not, such a marriage could actually become stronger and better than it was before and, through its own restoration, can show forth the grace of God to those who are going through the exact same thing. The world calls for divorce when a covenant is broken, but is that what God is saying? He needs examples of reconciliation; He needs examples of His restoration in a marriage to bring total victory and healing. He needs His people to begin to live the Word. As we live in the Word of God and forgive, He can restore, renew, revive, inspire and enlighten.

I am reminded of a couple that went through a terrible time in their marriage. They actually divorced and over time were reunited and now they are deeply in love with each other, and they minister to other couples to say that healing can happen and that God can put marriage back together. These are things that God's Word says He will do. He doesn't want us to be ashamed. He does not want us to be confound-ed. He said that those that put their trust in Him should be as Mt. Zion, they should not be ashamed and they should not be confounded. That means you needn't be confused or worried or troubled in your mind concerning issues and events in your life because His Word tells us that all things work together for good to them that love the Lord and to them that are the called according to His purpose. We have been called according to His purpose therefore all things will work together for our good.

There is one thing a ministering couple must not do. When a covenant has been broken, they must not pretend that everything is all right. You cannot go on with the ministry acting like everything's fine. You need to stop. You need to be healed. You need to be released from every foul spirit that has attached itself to your marriage. Break soul ties. Take some time and get someone to come in to carry on the ministry if you are pastoring. Cancel meetings if you are an evangelist. If you are on the mission field, come home. Take time for restoration. Restore this union, restore this marriage, and restore this love before you can go on trying to restore lives of others. That's like ministering with a bleeding heart, or ministering while undergoing open-heart surgery. You are susceptible to infection. I have observed too many people trying to carry on while they themselves are wounded. All they do is aggravate their condition. It's time to stop the bleeding, stop the infection, get healed, get whole, and then go forward in the will of God.

For couples whose covenant has been broken, true restoration usually strengthens trust. Be aware that trust takes time to be rebuilt. Don't hold things over one another's head. After apologies have been made, what more do you require? Simply pray for the offender and watch for signs of recovery and change. Go before the Lord; don't go to friends and neighbors, but go before the Lord. Ask Him to put mercy in your heart to give you what you truly need to trust your mate again. Look for signs of true repentance. Sometimes you encounter insincerity. I believe the Lord will allow you to see that. Trust must be earned again slowly. But when our spouse appears to be sincere in their heart and truly wants to make a change, we must go before the Lord and ask Him to give us the grace to trust this person again. Relax, and let God do His mighty work in both your hearts.

Denise S. Millben

7

The Common Enemy

As two silver trumpets, you must keep in mind that you have a common enemy; Satan and all of his demonic forces. He will use people to get to you, through words, looks, actions and deeds. Sometimes the people closest to you or that you thought supported you, are the ones that submit to demonic manipulation. There are often people who are not pleased that two trumpets are functioning according to the will of God. Depending on their spiritual state, it is likely that your obedience may have brought condemnation upon them and caused jealousy to creep into their heats, which in turn contaminated their motives. Unfortunately, not everybody wants to see your ministry flourish and develop. If you have two people dedicated to Almighty God, they soon become a target for Satan's devices.

One of Satan's strategies is to nullify or cancel out the plan of God. He does this through the "works of the flesh." If he can distract, discourage, or discredit you, he will. Often couples are faced with third party influences that are constantly interjecting ideas and thoughts that may or may not be beneficial to their marriage. The negative effects of such influences must be com-bated through fervent prayer and communication.

Once a young pastor's wife was feeling a little discouraged and she was crying in the church service and someone noticed and asked her what the problem was. She did not tell them she only replied, "just pray for me," and that person took her comment and added their thoughts to it and began to tell her that they had noticed that her husband was not very affectionate to her and that she seemed to be over worked, etcetera, etcetera, and before she knew it this person had dropped seeds of discord into her heart. This can happen so quickly and you must guard your heart.

Usually one partner notices something that is

wrong or something that is causing major upsets in the marriage. Rather than keeping it inside until some major eruption takes place, choose a time to quietly discuss the issues at hand. Deal with it with a godly Christian attitude. Remember, *"a soft answer turneth away wrath but grievous words stireth up anger."* There may be people who think they understand what your sound is or should be, therefore they offer input. What is most important is that the two silver trumpets agree to continually communicate with each other and continually agree to seek God for His direction.

As you have your private prayer and Bible reading time separately, always remember to share a thought or an idea with your spouse if the Spirit has given one to you. An active, rich, and consistent prayer life will strengthen your individual sounds and the sound will become more fine-tuned as you yield to God on a daily basis. Now that you are married to each other, your bond should be getting stronger and stronger, not weaker and weaker. Take practical steps to strengthen that bond.

Many couples sadly enter the ministry totally ignorant of the operation of the two trumpets. Their ignorance can sabotage their marriage and their ministry. They use other marriages and ministries as an example or template for their marriage and many times they are incorrect in their assessment of someone else's situation. I know it is much easier to look to people for examples but ultimately you must look to Jesus Christ for the blueprint for your life and marriage. The fact of the matter is you can never be 100% like someone else. Just be who you are. That is not to say that you can't benefit from the fine qualities others model before you. You can decide to adopt one or more of these qualities into your own marriage, but always remember the difference between principle and practice. A Biblical principle is an underlying idea or concept that the Bible puts forth as a necessity. The practice is the way in which they implement the principle in their own time and cultural setting.

For example, a couple might engage in the following practice; Every Monday morning, they go out for breakfast together and spend time talking and listening to each other's goals, dreams, and even complaints. Another couple may observe the first couple each Monday and try to imitate their practice. But instead of talking and listening to each other, they may invite an-other couple or bring a book or newspaper to the table and read or talk to others during the breakfast. They assume that they have followed the first couple's example. They might then become frustrated because they have not benefited by the same positive results. But they would fail to realize that, although they mimicked the successful couple's activity (practice), they failed to fulfill their underlying principle, which was to stimulate greater intimacy and trust in their relationship. Their (model couple) Monday ritual was a deliberate attempt to set aside quality time to actively listen to one another and enjoy one another's company. The second couple merely initiated a practice minus the principle. Establish your own principle and then initiate a practice to accomplish it. Just be yourself.

Ministering couples need constant updates on the vision. Ministering couples need to be open and up front. They need to be free from fear.

Plan to go on a date at least twice monthly. This date should be planned and should last at least two to three hours. Tell each other positive things. Don't talk shop. I once read a book about suggested discussion starters for couples to use just to help get the ball rolling. It is amazing how much the ministry is in your life and you will be tempted to talk about the ministry and other things that really does not provide a time of relaxation but actually a time of more stress. There are interesting things that you might not know about your spouse and conversation starters might help. Also make sure each one of you share; don't allow your conversation to be one-sided.

Present a united front before other people. Travel together as much as possible. Sit together when possible in worship service. Support each other with your presence and every other form of encouragement. After they minister, tell them that they did a good job. Appreciate them publicly and privately. After my husband preaches, I usually tell him what a blessing that message was to me. I never give him criticism before I have given him praise. He will often tell me that the way God used me was a blessing to him and then he might give me corrective comments.

The enemy will also use other people to try to get between the silver trumpets. It is the will of God to rescue many souls through you. What could happen to the "many" souls you are supposed to help if you allow your reputation to be ruined or your integrity imputed? It is not a wise thing for one of the trumpets to routinely travel to conferences, workshops, and other meetings without the other trumpet. When you travel alone all the time, or even frequently, you give a place for Satan to create a situation that could compromise your marriage and ministry.

Example: A man full of God and full of integrity

travels alone to a conference. The wife stays at home. Their marriage is solid; however, there are women who are not full of God and do not have integrity who attend conferences for the sole purpose of ensnaring an unsuspecting person. No, it won't happen the very first time you go alone, but if you allow it to become a habit, you are setting yourself up for disaster. I can speak from personal experience. I attended a conference many years ago. My husband was unable to come along (we usually travel together) so I went with a sister from my assembly. While in church, a preacher complemented me on the way I smelled, my hair, my looks in general, my voice. He then asked me if I was married. I told him, yes, and then prominently displayed my wedding band. He then proceeded to ask me out for dinner after service. Now that did it! I told him no! He then pressed on, undaunted, and asked me if I were happily married, to which I replied "YES!" While this was taking place, we were sitting in a worship service. I immediately began to pray for another seat, because I re-solved to move. After the offering, he said he would be back and he left. He never came back to that seat for the rest of the service. Praise God!! Can you see how easily someone could be ensnared and entrapped? "Be sober, be vigilant because your adversary the devil is walking about in the earth seeking whom he may devour." It's good to introduce your spouse if they are present. Even if they are not present, acknowledge them in their absence. Talk about them briefly in a loving tone but only if you mean it. This will be your first line of defense. Travel with another person of the same sex. This will discourage people from drawing wrong conclusions about you.

Footnote: People will talk about you if you are about Kingdom work. We will be the topic of conservations, so please understand that. My point is don't give people ammunition to use against you. Ministering couples have to deal with enough "stuff" without bringing on un-necessary problems. Try to close doors before anything comes issuing forth.

It is important for couples to spend time together and talk, talk, talk, laugh, laugh, laugh. Enjoy each other. There will be time to discuss the ministry issues, but reserve time for each other. Look for innovative ways to spend time together, i.e. board games, golf, reading to each other, crossword puzzles, listening to music together, exercising together. Engage in any kind of mutual interest outside of your ministry.

Two Silver Trumpets

8

Knowing

Dwell with your trumpet according to knowledge. The knowing is a level of intimacy that every couple must strive to achieve. We casually make statements like "It's been a pleasure knowing you," or we may think we know them, when actually you just met them or, at most, you have spoken with them on a few occasions. You may have worked with someone and, based on that association, you assert that you know them. You may be acquainted with them, but **knowing** requires intimacy.

Intimacy knows the other person so deeply and so

thoroughly that you know things about that person that no one else knows. Many times when intimacy is mentioned, people think of it only in sexual terms. Of course intimacy does include the sexual act; however, intimacy encompasses much more than a physical act. It involves touching someone's spirit. It involves being able to tap into their heart and feel it beating in sync with your heart. It involves hearing their cry and feeling their pain within your own spirit.

Intimacy begins with questioning the smallest, most minute details of the person. It requires studying. Study the person, study every move, and study every look. Know how they will react to a sad song or a corny joke. Study their moods; understand what makes them tick.

The knowing requires hours of unspoken observation, hours of spoken communication, sensitivity to their smallest need, and a yearning to meet that need.

You might ask the question, how do I do that? Knowing begins with holding hands or putting arms around each other, feeling the pulse and heartbeat of the other, and listening to their heart. To be intimate, you must open up, and in order for someone to open up there must be an atmosphere of safety and security. I will open up to you if I know you will guard my heart.

Share the smallest of things. Share pet names for each other. Share glances. Many married couples in ministry never achieve intimacy because it requires time and some are so busy ministering that they don't realize the need for intimacy with their spouse.

There needs to be time set aside for just the two of you. The time should not be compromised by phone calls or visits. Give each other messages and tell your earliest memories. If these memories are painful, share a little at a time. Many times, just knowing what someone else knows what you have gone through is comforting, even if you feel helpless in the mending of these painful memories, just having someone there and listening can bring ultimate healing. Intimacy takes time. The Knowing takes time.

This is a subject very few ministering couples discuss due to the private nature of the subject matter, so allow me to offer suggestions to assist in the intimacy that is needed so desperately in this age.

In many marriages, one of the partners has found intimacy with someone else. Maybe they never had sexual relations, but they share information that was very sensitive and very personal. They created an environment of safety and the knowing drew them in. Be careful.

Couples in ministry need to know each other more than anyone else because of the position they are in. Outward demonstrations of affections are fine as long as they are genuine and not just for show. Make deliberate and conscious efforts to truly touch one another. Some couples touch, but it is unconscious and without meaning or feeling. It's like petting the dog. But there is a different feeling communicated with a deliberate touch. The touch lets the partner know I've been thinking about you. I want to feel you close to me. This speaks volumes to the spouse. Use words of endearment. Words you don't call anyone else. These are **our** words. They mean you and I belong exclusively to one another.

In the ministry, I understand that there are tremendous demands on your life and time but spontaneous and unplanned activities create a bond between you. Make memories. Have a picnic in your bedroom on the floor. Tell each other funny jokes. Take a bubble bath together in a candle-lit room with soft music. Speak words of strength and hope.

Someone reading this might say this is not what spiritually strong ministers do. They pray and read and fast. I will agree that praying, reading and fasting are very much a part of a spiritual ministry, but you do not pray every waking moment, and if you don't start doing some of the things suggested here, you will need to pray even more because your spouse will have drifted away from you.

Intimacy is a desire of every one of us. The desire to be close and share and receive is critical. Being intimate with your spouse is spiritual. Knowing is obeying God's word. Put little special notes in special places, like on the pillow or on the mirror, in their briefcase or suitcase. Each little message says, I love you, and need you. My husband always says "I love you more than I need you and I need you for always"- that means a lot to me. Have prolonged kisses in-stead of those pecks on the cheeks before you leave and go anywhere. Have prolonged hugs. Kisses and hugs say volumes when you "know." Foot massages, back rubs. Lie in each other's arms and read a book together. Give yourself to each other. Intimacy should bring you to passionate, intense encounters. Shame left when knowing came. Don't be ashamed of your body.

Knowing during lovemaking is very important. You need to communicate likes and dis-likes and those should be respected. True intimacy knows. Some couples don't achieve true intimacy because they don't discuss their likes and dislikes during their most private and intimate times together. Talk, encourage, and tell them when they have ignited the fires of passion. This will help both of you. Create an atmosphere that is absent from fear, pain, and dread. Make sure you are clean and smell good. Make a memory that is mutually acceptable. Spontaneity is exciting; not every sexual encounter needs to be planned. To keep the fire burning in your marriage, don't allow sex to become routine or merely a duty. God gave us these wonder feelings. It is not wrong to enjoy them with your spouse as often as you like and for as long as you like, and anywhere that is private.

These intimate private times are personal and should not be shared unless you get permission from the spouse to share. Please don't negate the intimacy by telling the conversations or acts that are exclusively yours. If you do, it will be very difficult to regain that level of intimacy and trust again.

Marriage is honorable and the bed undefiled. Don't use sex as a weapon against your spouse or a manipulative tool to get what you want. Let love abound and love in kind. Bring God into every aspect of your marriage and at every level. He will strengthen and settle you. Press toward intimacy; that is the deep rich heart of a marriage.

Denise S. Millben

    This book has by no means exhausted every aspect of marriage and ministry; however, it was my desire to give you something to assist you in building a life that brings glory to God. I pray that when the Master sends a command to **Blow the Trumpet in Zion**, that you will be ready for service.

Two Silver Trumpets

9

Silence is not Golden

A Practical Guide for Couples in Ministry

There are two places where people should be safe one is at home and the other is at church. Many things are happening in the world today that makes being in a safe place a very important thing. Slapping, hitting, biting, grabbing, kicking, spitting, and shoving are not the ways to express yourself to your mate nor is a way to be treated in your home by your mate. This is one of the hardest chapters I have written because this is something that is so hush hush in families but it is leaking over into the church. Some of the people in the church are living double lives. They are sweet and kind to people at church but they are horrible and nasty to their family members at home. They are living like Doctor Jekyll and Mr. Hyde. By day they are wonderful but at night they turn into another kind of person. One you would not recognize. The bad thing is that sometimes these people are found in the homes of church leaders.

What? Physical abuse found in the church? Yes!!! What? Mental and emotional abuse in the church? Yes!!!!

Many homes that have abuse going on can really be the best looking family in the church. Sometimes the most involved and the most giving people in the congregation. It is hard because I have known of an abusive husband and at the time neither I nor my husband really knew what to do. There were accusations made about the husband by the wife, but we did not know what to say or do. We prayed yes but there had to be more that we should have done. In retrospect I realized that I needed to be there for the abused spouse. I needed to offer her an alternative place to stay and give advice as to what she needed to do.

I was very naïve when it came to what goes on in the homes of the people. I thought that everyone lived like I did, but the more I became exposed to the lives of others I noticed that people did not live like I did.

What goes on behind closed doors is astonishing to me. This portion of the book is going to expose the signs and give you some sound advice on the way to deal with your abuser and what you should do to deal with the abuse. Abuse should not be allowed because this is not pleasing to the Lord.

Definition of abuse is the physical or sexual maltreatment of a person, the improper use or illegal harmful use of someone or something, insults or improper language directed to a person.

An abuser can be a man or woman, a deacon, Sunday school teacher, a pastor, a worship leader or youth leader because of the nature of this book I am speaking primarily to ministering couples.

First I am speaking the words of Apostle Paul when he said, "let it not be once named among you." The sad truth is that is named among us. This is not acceptable. God does not condone this behavior but there is good news, there is hope for you and there is help for you if you want to stop. The first step is to recognize that hitting your spouse is wrong and should not happen in your home or anywhere else. Your home should be one of the safest places in the world. When your home is not safe where can you go to be safe? The atmosphere in your home should be one of peace and harmony. When that is challenged there are ways to regain the peace in your home and hitting and slapping is not the way to do it. If you recognize there are anger issues in yourself or your spouse, get HELP! The help can be counseling but it should also include deliverance. The power of God is great but we have to acknowledge that we need his help.

There are too many spouses going through the motions at church because of the home conditions. When you pretend that you are okay just to save face you are not helping yourself or your spouse. Truth is what is necessary in any relationship. You do not have to make the person out to be the villain but you will need to talk to someone that can help you and give you Godly counsel. To be silent, grin and bear it is not what is best for you, your spouse or your family. If children are involved they are observing negative behavior and the modeling they are watching is showing them the wrong way to solve problems.

Living a life of deception and lies is not the abundant life that Jesus spoke of in His word. Some of the lies that the devil whispers in the minds of people that are living in an abusive situation are;

1. No one will believe you.

2. What did you do to deserve this?

3. What if he/she leaves, how will you make it?

4. Maybe he/she will change.

5. If you do everything they want then they will treat me better.

6. It's not so bad.

7. Does God see this? If he does why doesn't he stop the madness?

8. If you tell someone and then he/she changes those you tell will hold it against them.

9. God wants us to forgive and move on.

10. You are being strong.

11. You love him/her and you made a promise before God...for better or for worst.

12. You are all alone in this trouble.

13. You will be embarrassed.

14. *You are scared.*

15. *You don't want to be alone.*

16. *Friends and family will side with the other person.*

17. *You are good at containing and holding it together.*

18. *Anyone can leave but who stays to show strength.*

19. *There is something wrong with you.*

20. *This is the way things are in ministry homes.*

21. *It's not always bad.*

    My brother and sister please remember that the enemy of your marriage is engaged in perpetual dialogue that accuses the brethren. (Revelations 12:10) Learning how to stop the dialogue in your thoughts is very important. Each day you need to speak the word of God aloud so that your ears hear your mouth declare what God says about you and your life.

    This chapter is dealing with a very touchy subject of abuse. You will need to wrap yourself in the grace of God and humility to be changed. We have heard many talk show hosts deal with the subject of spousal abuse but it is rarely discussed among ministry couples, but the sad fact is that there is a silence about this topic and no one wants to address.

Fear and embarrassment are the main factors that have allowed this culprit to remain hidden and unopposed. There are several types of abuse and many times people are not aware of the subtle signs of abuse.

The sad thing is that couples that are engaged in abuse really do not feel they have anyone to talk to. Threats cause the abused spouse to keep silent about the issues, thus preventing the family from getting the help that is desperately needed.

Here is an example of signs of abuse. There are ministering couples who really don't realize that some of the behaviors they are engaged in is abuse. Pulling hair and yanking arms and limbs to get the persons attention is abusive behavior.

The saddest thing I have heard is a deacon and wife who are very active in their church. The deacon is always working around the church, "Johnny on the spot" for every event, but at home he is a totally different person. He is all smiles at church and in front of people. Mr. Personality, full of complements and helpful in every way but the moment he gets into the car the smile disappears and the criticisms begin. The wife sits in silence while an avalanche of hurtful words bombard her and escalates until by the time they reach their home he is yelling, slamming doors, critical of the home setting. If the wife tries to defend her position by speaking it is like throwing gasoline on a blazing inferno. He goes to a new level of rage and maybe he is only verbally abusive, but many times it graduates from words to hitting, grabbing, pushing, shoving etc. No one should be treated in such a manner. This is a child of God as well as your spouse.

In I Corinthians it reads, *"That husbands and wives should submit to each other."* A marriage should exemplify Christ and His Church. King David stated that *"he was young and now old and he had never seen the righteous forsaken nor his seed begging bread."* Christ takes good care of His bride. He actually gives His angels charge over us to keep us, with that level of love and care and concern you can be sure He will not abuse His bride. We must be like Jesus. Abuse is unacceptable in a Godly home. There are many kinds of abuse.

Physical; this is when a person is hit, slapped, kicked, pushed, shaken, spit on, pinched, hair yanked, deprived of food, water, clothing, stomped, poked, confined, bitten, doused, submerged, burned, whipped, cut, etc.

Verbal; yelling, screaming, threatening, hollering, name calling, extended silence, whispered threats, degrading words, put downs, embarrassing words, exposing words, etc.

Mental; put downs, comparing with others, fear, smiling while saying" you can't make it without me", constantly saying you are nothing, hurting you then buying you a gift, you cannot do anything right, telling others in public what a wonderful person you are, then at home say you are nothing, stating your faults all the time, holding your failures over you by reminding you of them daily, etc.

I believe there is spiritual abuse. That is where the abusing spouse uses spiritual matters as a battering ram. i.e. "God told me...I hear the voice of God daily what about you?" God gives me dreams and visions that come to pass; I know the Hebrew and Greek meaning of all important words which gives me a deeper knowledge of spiritual truths. You need to be more spiritual. You need to pray more like me. I hear from God and you don't so you cannot tell me anything and everything I say comes from God, so you cannot dispute it.

Wanting "us time" is not spiritual and it is selfish. If you express wanting time to have fun you have missed the voice of God. Statements like these are spiritually abusive and cause the other spouse to doubt their relationship with God and His work. Remember you are "Two Silver Trumpets" and you have different sounds but made of one piece of silver. Your worth is the same it's just the function that is different.

Don't be the cause of your spouse pulling away from God and His plan for their lives because they are trying to live up to your standard of spirituality. This is wrong and if you find yourself here, "Stop It!"

I am a firm believer that when you see things in the newspaper, magazines, television and internet, you need to pay attention. It is going to infiltrate church going families.

Spousal abuse is taking place in the world and it grieves me to say that it is also taking place in the church. It can be considered the silent killer. We don't take note of it until something big hits the newsstand or goes out over the World Wide Web. Headlines like, "pastor's wife shoots and kills husband," or "pastor shoots himself and commits suicide after killing wife and children".

These headlines cause us to look for a brief moment and then dismiss this behavior as some remote isolated act by some deranged person with mental issues, but the truth of the matter is that many things lead up to these extreme acts. The people you think you know well could be under this kind of abuse and they feel helpless, alone and desperate. People in ministry have a double whammy, they are expected to be perfect and when they are not they are given no help and no grace.

Therefore many suffer in silence. They put on a mask of pretense at church. If asked, "how are you doing?" The response is "fine, blessed, great", because many times that is what is expected and the image cannot be ruined with spots and blemishes.

Let's keep the unflawed image going. Let's pretend we are happy. I will continue to let you pretend to be a Godly man while you abuse me at home because I have no other choice. Let me say this right now, "You have other choices." Stop the madness! Will it be easy? "No!" But you must find someone you trust to confide in. Preferably someone outside of the assemble you minister in. Get a diligent prayer partner, not a talk only partner, but someone who will pray with you and for you. Prayer is a powerful tool in your arsenal. After you have fortified yourself with prayer go to the highest level of spiritual covering you have. I say this because normally it would be your pastor but if the pastor is the abuser you need to go above him or her for help and support. Silence is not golden in this case.

If the care for leaders is not present in your assembly find a place that will help them out of their decline. A place that will allow them to open up and share, knowing they will be surrounded and counseled and cared for until the necessary changes are firmly in place. Frankly in the church world many are so busy that they really don't want to know what is really going on. That might mean additional time to work with the couple. God forbid that we get too busy to help a couple in trouble.

I hope this chapter will ruffle feathers and stir some people to action. The intent is to allow you to come face to face with real issues and now that you see it clearly do something about it.

There are pastors who are brought face to face with abuse in their congregation and they might not know what to do. That is possible, but please don't do nothing. Doing nothing is subjecting one of God's precious little ones to something that you would not want your own child to go through.

I know of a young pastor who was called into an abusive situation. The husband was out going and quite talented, got along with everyone in the church but the secret life was one of spousal abuse. The wife was silent for a while and finally one evening there was a violent outbreak and the pastor was called. Upon arrival the altercation was over. The pastor talked to both parties and asked the husband to get into his car and they went for a ride to help him cool off. They prayed but he was allowed to return home. "Wrong!" The abuser needs to find somewhere else to stay. The pastor needed to reassure the abused that first he believes them, secondly they can trust him and thirdly he will get help for both of them if they are willing.

Now I am going to say something right here that will cause a stir. Don't encourage the abused to stay in the house. Provide some other living arrangements for the abuser so the abused feels safe. I recommend deliverance, anger management classes and counseling sessions for the abuser before the abuser is allowed to return home. This may take some time but it will be worth it to save a marriage and lives.

Give the people hope that they will be under girded and supported until there is a change. That means we are in this for the long haul. Exposure is one

of the deterrents to abuse. *Remember "Silence is not Golden"*

Denise S. Millben

DEVOTIONAL

COUPLES IN MINISTRY

DENISE S. MILLBEN

FOREWORD

God walks with us in our daily encounters with the situations and circumstances of our lives *(Psalms 119: 105)*. Through them, we learn to use His word to overcome challenges one day at a time and to celebrate victories brought through trusting in His guidance.

The author of *"Two Silver Trumpets"*, Pastor Denise Millben is an example of one person who has grown and succeeded in life through daily walking in God's word and prayerfully trusting in His guidance.

Not many people possess the ability to make things practical and understandable. Many leaders, in fact do just the opposite. I believe the reason God chose Pastor Denise to write *"Two Silver Trumpets"* is because He knew she would embody what it says and she does. I have observed firsthand her ability to apply deeply spiritual truths in practical ways. I have listened to her teach, pray and minister with depth and accuracy. I have sat across from her in meetings as she shared practical wisdom concerning difficult problems. Simply stated, she is a gift to the body of Christ. Through this devotional you now have the opportunity and blessing of experiencing this gift yourself. Not only is this devotional practical, but it is also timely.

Two Silver Trumpets will transform and renew your spirit as you allow God's word to refresh and reshape your thinking. Allow the word of God to encourage your heart as you believe God rather than circumstances. Follow Pastor Denise as she takes you on a 30-day spiritual journey as you are encouraged to believe God for the impossible. Most of all, apply these nuggets shared as principles for your assured victory in your daily life. This devotional is a must have for every leader who has the desire to move forward in ministry. If you have experienced a crisis in your faith, I encourage you to use this devotional prayerfully. I am confident that it will bring out the Godly values so evident in its author. It is my hope that, through these devotionals, God will "shape the ordering of your lives," "encourage the work of your hands," and "graciously equip you with faith, hope and genuine love for the call of God on your life." May the Lord richly bless you as you become the *Best Servant Leader* for the Kingdom.

Marye E. Jones

Two Silver Trumpets

1
A SERVANTS HEART

For, brethren, ye have been called unto liberty; only use not liberty for an occasion to the flesh, but by love serve one another.

Galatians 5:13, KJV

Serving; what an interesting concept in the church today. Serving is a rare commodity that requires humility. It works well *only* when you don't think of yourself more highly than you ought to (see Romans 12:3).

Having a servant's heart should be a high priority when ministering to the saints of the Most High God! A servant's heart serves without looking for accolades from others. A servant's heart seeks to help and render assistance without looking for repayment, knowing that the reward comes from our heavenly Father.

As servants of the Lord, we are called to work with people whom God has called or is calling to become His servants, as well. We are called to serve one another. However, when you understand that you are a servant of the Lord—and not the people—it becomes very freeing.

You are a servant of the Lord, and one thing you should know about Him is that He is not an abuser. In fact, He is a good paymaster. To serve the Lord and to be in His employ produces great benefits. Serving the Lord might seem like a lowly path, and serving people can seem like a thankless task; but rest assured that God is taking note of every effort, and He is recording all your labors of love. He will not allow you to serve and come up empty-handed.

We are servants and not slaves. There is a huge difference. A slave does not have any rights. Slaves are not allowed to think for themselves. A slave does not get pay for all the hard work he does. A slave is not allowed to think or exercise any personal attempts to rise. Slaves are not encouraged to move forward. There are no incentives to do their best. They operate under an oppressive system that often leads to depression or despair.

A servant, however, is free to go and come as he pleases as long as the work gets done. A servant is valued for the skills and the talents he brings to the job. A servant is given a task and then allowed to think through the process and come up with a plan to accomplish his task. A servant receives benefits or special rewards for a job well done.

Jesus Christ was the ultimate servant. He served people even when He knew they were plotting to kill Him. He kept one purpose in mind: pleasing the Father. For the joy that was set before Him, Jesus endured the cross and despised the shame; and while we were yet sinners Christ died for us (see Hebrews 12:2; Romans 5:8).

Serve with a smile and with the armor of the Lord. Decide to be the best servant that you can be in the name of the Lord. It pays well!

2
SPEAK IT AND BELIEVE IT

So Jesus answered and said to them, "Assuredly, I say to you, if you have faith and do not doubt, you will not only do what was done to the fig tree, but also if you say to this mountain, 'Be removed and be cast into the sea,' it will be done. And whatever things you ask in prayer, believing, you will receive."

Matthew 21:21-22; NKJV

Doubting is a natural human characteristic. However, when you are born again, a significant character change takes place.

Once you are born "from above," you receive a seed of faith (see John 3:3; 1 Peter 1:23). As that faith is cultivated by the Word of God, it should develop to a level that supernaturally empowers believers. Jesus said that if you have faith and do not doubt, you can to speak to a fig tree and cause it never to bear fruit again.

He goes on to say that not only can you do that, but you can speak to a mountain and it will have to obey you.

There have been interpretations suggesting that the fig tree represents a religious system that must come down. I am not here to debate that point. Let's focus not so much on the item being removed as the power in the words of a person with faith to remove it. When you walk in that level of faith, whatever you ask in prayer you will receive, when you pray according to God's will.

We want the testimony that mountain-moving faith is what we possess as sons and daughters of the Most High God. Push the old doubting nature away and fully grasp the new nature—because along with it comes an incredible realm where nothing is impossible. Only agree with God and you shall have whatsoever you say.

Listen, my friend, the Holy Word of God says that *you* can speak to this mountain. Don't stop until *you* get there. Whether it's a physical mountain, a spiritual mountain, an emotional mountain, a systemic mountain—it really doesn't matter. The only thing that matters is that your faith can move it out of the way.

I know you have heard many sermons on faith and what faith can do. But I want you to consider the fact that we can hear powerful sermons, and even preach powerful sermons, and not really walk in what we hear on a daily basis.

Admit that you are not there, but you want to get there. Start now. Go ahead; ask God for that level of faith.

Today is the day that you must declare in your own spirit: "Jesus, this faith that you are speaking about in your Word is the faith I want to activate in my life! I want to be that believer that speaks to mountains and they move."

Now pray this with me: "Dear Lord Jesus, I ask you to release the level of faith that will move mountains in my life and in the lives of others. And give me the grace to operate in humility and love. In Jesus' name. Amen!"

3
I AM

And God said to Moses, "I AM WHO I AM." And He said, "Thus you shall say to the children of Israel, 'I AM has sent me to you.'"

Exodus 3:14; NKJV

The name *Yahweh* (or *Jehovah*) is a form of the Hebrew verb that means "to be" and is translated "I AM," "The Present One," and "He Who Is." The encouragement and strength that comes from knowing that God is "The Great I AM" will empower you at your darkest moment.

There may be times when it feels like the walls are closing in; and even when people around you are trying to encourage you, somehow their words do not help in your time of need. You can be in the middle of friends and family but still feel like you are alone on a deserted island.

"I AM" is with you—that is the comforting word you

need, and it is a word of encouragement. Remember, God is "a very present help in time of trouble" (Psalm 46:1).

"I AM" is here and He will never leave. Remember He is with you right now while you are reading this devotional. He refers to Himself as "The Present One," and He is with you in your time of pain, loneliness, suffering, worry, grief, and disappointment.

The enemy of your soul does not want you to grasp the fact that our God is omnipresent because he wants you to stay in a dark place. But God says, "I will never leave you nor forsake you" (Hebrews 13:5). As you remember that you are *not* alone, you can come out in the name of Jesus.

Come on now, believe. "I AM" can:
(You fill in the blank and stand on God's promise.)

Let's pray:
> "Dear Jesus, You are the only one who always keeps His promises. I thank You right now for Your grace and help in this time of need. I need Your help to come out of this place where I feel so isolated and separated from everyone and everything. I go through the motions, but really deep inside I am fearful and troubled. Please lift me up where I belong. Lift me up in You where there is never a lonely moment. I trust You. In Jesus' name. Amen!"

4
ABUNDANT LIFE

The thief does not come except to steal, and to kill, and to destroy. I have come that they may have life, and that they may have it more abundantly.

John 10:10; NKJV

Life is so precious. Unfortunately, as responsible church leaders, we can frequently miss out on the wonderful moments in everyday life that happen suddenly and without notice. We must be careful not to miss these moments because they cannot be reclaimed.

Sometimes, we need a not-so-gentle reminder: "Hey, church leader, stop a minute and go for a walk with your spouse! Do something relaxing that does not relate to church work." It amazes me that many leaders don't know how or when to take a break, or how to relax and enjoy their surroundings.

I encourage you to pace yourself and allow time in your schedule to enjoy the rain falling on the roof or watch the sunset or count a few thousand stars. Your heavenly Father made them all. He created the world, and He meant for us to enjoy His creation. Go ahead; it won't cost you a dime and could really be worth millions to you and to your family.

You don't have to go on vacation far away. That might not fit into your budget. But you can take a neighborhood vacation, fly a kite in the park, stroll along the bank of a river, or go for a walk and use binoculars to see how many species of birds or types of flowers you can identify.

Spontaneous fun is what you need today. Have a carpet picnic in the living room with your family. Make paper airplanes and fly them in the house. If you live in an area of the country where there is snow, go outside and make a snowman or have a snowball fight with the family. Come inside and have hot chocolate with marshmallows and laugh at all the crazy things you just did.

It has come to my attention that many church leaders get so caught up with the daily routine and the emergencies of ministry that they fail to enjoy life and they forget the reason that Jesus came. Enjoying life brings glory to God because He is the life-giver. Jesus said, "I am come that they might have life and that more abundantly."

Take time to stop and smell the roses, stare at the moon, contemplate a sunset, watch the tide roll in, look at a newborn baby's fingers, listen to the birds in your yard, look for a four-leaf clover, run through the rain and stomp in the puddles, eat an ice cream cone from the bottom, or snuggle in front of a fire. Come on; do something that requires your attention but is not stressful.

Life is beautiful and short. Enjoy it, and bring glory to God!

5
COMPASSION

But when He saw the multitudes, He was moved with compassion for them, because they were weary and scattered, like sheep having no shepherd.

Matthew 9:36, NKJV

There may be times when, as a leader in the church, you might become jaded by the various situations and personality types you encounter in the ministry. Resist the temptation to lump all of God's people together in the same category. Remember that people are not the same and that you need to pray as you deal with each individual and circumstance.

Jesus saw that the people who followed Him were faint and scattered abroad like sheep without a shepherd. He knew that in this life there are many things that can press upon people until they feel faint. That is not the time for them to be treated harshly. They are already whipped by the world, and they need to be shown the Father's compassion.

The most important thing to keep in mind is that God loves His people tremendously. Jesus died for every one of the people to whom you minister. He gave His life for them. Therefore, to minister effectively, you must step into the love of Jesus. This must be done outside of yourself. Compassion is a family trait that comes from our Father in heaven.

For various reasons, we can come to the end of our rope when dealing with members of the body of Christ. Some people are willful and won't listen to wisdom and counsel. Others refuse to seek counsel prior to making decisions; then, when things go wrong, they want you to help them fix the mess they made. You might be tempted to say in your mind, "I could have saved you from this disaster if you had only come to me first." But, because compassion is a family trait, you will be moved by the compassion that your heavenly Father has for all of His beloved.

Just as God had more compassion on you than you deserved, extend the same level of love and compassion to the people that have been placed into your care. No matter how many times they cry, you can be moved by their need and do whatever is within your power to help, comfort, guide, and rescue them.

Deal with each situation based on its own merit. Each person is different, and each person is loved by God. You want to be able to say to the Father that you cherished the precious sheep that He entrusted into your care.

6
HIS SPECIAL PEOPLE

But you are a chosen generation, a royal priesthood, a holy nation, His own special people, that you may proclaim the praises of Him who called you out of darkness into His marvelous light.

I Peter 2:9; NKJV

First Peter 2:9 describes the heritage of every believer. Knowing who you are and *whose* you are is paramount in this spiritual walk. But sometimes the days roll into weeks, the weeks roll into months, one situation transitions into another, and before you know it you are burdened down with care and seemingly without strength to go on.

Occasionally, you might be tempted to avoid the things the enemy brings into your life. We have been given everything that pertains to life and godliness (see 2 Peter 1:3). But when the issues of life begin to compound, we often shirk from our duties as good soldiers of Christ. You might be tempted to believe that if you remain under the radar and don't agitate the enemy, then maybe he would leave you alone. But that is not the case.

The enemy of our souls is happy when we, as born again believers, do not respond to him with the authority given to us by our Lord and Savior. There is a way to deal with the onslaught of the enemy. Yelling, crying, screaming, and fussing will not deter him. You must realize that you have the power to confront the enemy and force him to take his hands off you and your family.

Listen, you are a child of the King of kings through your new birth and you are powerful through the Spirit by faith in Christ. Remember that the Word of God is quick and powerful (see Hebrews 4:12). You have all of heaven backing you when you pray the Word and speak the Word into your situation.

You can say something like this:
"I come in the name of the resurrected Jesus, whose I am and whom I serve. God's Word says, 'That at the name of Jesus every knee should bow, of things in heaven, and things in earth, and things under the earth, and that every tongue should confess that Jesus Christ is Lord' (Philippians 2:10-11, KJV).

"I take up the whole armor of God and stand against the wiles of the devil. I put on the helmet of salvation to remind me of the great price that was paid by Jesus. He invested all to purchase my salvation, and what He did will remain in effect until the end of the age. I have the breastplate of righteousness. My loins are girded with truth. My feet are covered, and I am prepared to run and spread the gospel of peace. I take up the shield of faith and the sword of the Spirit, which is the Word of God (see Ephesians 6:10-18).

"In the name of Jesus, I take authority over this conglomeration of spiritual attacks and I command it to leave my home and my family."

In Christ, you have been given power to overcome the enemy (see Luke 10:19; 1 John 4:4). Come on! Walk in it and live in it. You have that kind of power to command the demonic forces to leave you alone and never come back!

7
BE STILL

Be still, and know that I am God; I will be exalted among the nations, I will be exalted in the earth!

Psalm 46:10; NKJV

In an overwhelmed moment, I responded to Psalm 46:10 by thinking, "What! How can I be still? I have so many things to do, places where I am needed, and people that require my attention. How could I possibly be still?"

If you knew my hectic schedule, you would understand why being still does not easily come to mind. There are so many things that I have to do. I have to care for my children; that is a responsibility that God has given to me. You cannot ignore a crying baby or a child who needs to finish homework assignments. There are lunches to prepare, parent teacher conferences to attend, sleepovers to host, and birthday parties to plan. Oh, and don't forget, my spouse needs attention! You cannot ignore your mate. They need conversation, attention, meals, intimate time, and laughs. Also, rooms need to be cleaned, garbage taken out, floors mopped, windows washed . . . . Need I go on?

You see, I'm not talking about responsibilities that I have picked up along the way. Good Samaritan activities would be nice, but they really can be done by someone else. I'm talking about those things that have to be done by me—those assignments that have my name stamped all over them. Who cares for our home? Me! Who cares for the projects that my boss has given to me? Me! Who handles the household jobs? Me! Who answers the phone? Me!

I know you are thinking, "But you don't have to answer the phone." However, you and I both know that there are some phone calls that cannot be ignored. So on that particular day when I read, "Be still," it was a request that seemed almost more than I could bear.

Have you ever had days like that? Have you had times when you read Psalm 46:10 and wondered, "When, where, and how, Lord?"

With our busy and sometimes nearly impossible schedules, we have to learn how to grab a "be still" moment here and there. This passage is not asking that we take an hour to go away and be still before God. In fact, we can be still by quieting our minds while we continue to work and move about. When we get a "be still" moment in the bathtub after a long day, that is good; but when we can't, we can snatch some time in the shower or stand by the kitchen counter and breathe a moment of "be still."

The admonishment in Psalm 46:10 is not just to "Be still," but to "Be still, and know that I am God." In every situation, you must remind yourself that God is in the mix of every decision, need, and pull in life. Take a minute and remind yourself that you are not in charge; God is! Knowing this is very important. Stop and remember that you cannot do anything without the Lord. You cannot fulfill all of the pressing needs of the day without the Lord.

Just take a moment and get still, and know that all of the multiplicity of things needed cannot be done without the help of our Lord. Breathe in His strength and His power to get the job done. This will bring glory to God; because when you are tempted to think of yourself as if you are a superhero, you immediately will say, "No, I know that God is my helper and that is why I have made it this far."

8
BENEFITS

Bless the LORD, O my soul, and forget not all His benefits.

Psalm 103:2, NKJV

The human mind is very interesting. It has been recorded in medical journals that people can experience such trauma that it causes them to forget segments of their lives. They actually block out the traumatic events. Although selective amnesia happens to some, it is rare. When you encounter something bad or distressing in your life, it is not common that you will forget it all. Unfortunately, many people are forced to remember, repeatedly think about, or relive painful events.

Psalm 103:2 encourages us to remember the Lord's benefits. This is an antidote to the negative memories that invade our minds.

First, you have to bless the Lord. Blessing the Lord is speaking of His goodness and applauding His wonderful character. Just begin to bless the Lord God Almighty: "God I call you my healer, and I call you the lily of the valley. I call you my anchor, strong tower, Savior, and redeemer. You are love. You are the chief cornerstone. You are the great I Am."

After you bless the Lord in your soul—which is your will, your imagination, and your emotions—the memory bank is unlocked, and you can begin to recall all His benefits.

A benefit is an addition to your salary. In the natural world, a benefit is life and health insurance, a company car, a company credit card, a big corner office with a view, free tuition reimbursement, professional development perks, a 401(k) or 403(b) retirement plan, investment shares, a company laptop or cell phone, paid vacation, a chauffeur, paid sick leave, long- and short-term disability, survivor benefits, and pension. Translate all of these previously mentioned benefits into your spiritual walk.

The benefits, besides salvation, include but are not limited to:

- Health insurance—by His strips we are healed (see Isaiah 53:5).
- Life insurance—He promised to be with us even unto death and will give us eternal life (see Matthew 28:20; John 10:28).
- Protection—He gives his angels charge over us to keep us in all our ways (see Psalm 91:11).
- Direct access to the throne room—He told us to call him any time and he will hear us (see Hebrews 4:16).
- Angelic assistance—the ministering spirits are for the believers (see Hebrews 1:14).
- Victory over the enemy—He has given us demon routing power (see Luke 10:19; 2 Corinthians 10:4).
- Open line to the King of kings—He is a constant companion to us all (see Psalm 91:15).
- A great payback plan—no one has given up things for the kingdom that the Father will not give it back to him (see Mark 10:29-30).

When negative thoughts abound and you are having difficulty remembering all His benefits, you can start by blessing the Lord.

9
HANDPICKED

Take what is yours and go your way. I wish to give to this last man the same as to you. Is it not lawful for me to do what I wish with my own things? Or is your eye evil because I am good?'

Matthew 20:14-15, NKJV

Upon reading this wonderful passage and its context from God's Holy Word, a feeling of jubilation should spring up in your heart. Even though Matthew 20:14-15 was not written to us, it was written and preserved *for* us.

The spiritual implications are almost too wonderful to contain. The owner of the vineyard represents the Lord Jesus Christ. He was looking for workers to hire. Several agreed to work for Him, and they considered it an honor to have been chosen to join His workforce.

Think about this: the great God of glory handpicked each one of us to serve in His vineyard. We are the ones who came later in the day. We have worked hard for the Master, but we have not experienced what the workers earlier in the day have had to endure. Praise be to God!

He handpicked the other laborers before us. There were those who labored and toiled through much adversity and hardships. They worked in the heat of the day. And even through the enemy's attacks, they pressed on.

When you get a little tired from the effort you've expended for the Lord, just remember there are others who have been working longer and through greater adversity. I think that instead of complaining, we ought to say, "Thank you Lord for even considering me to be a co-laborer in your vineyard."

Here is the good part of this parable. The master paid the workers who came late on the scene the same as those who had been working all day. What an encouraging thought. We, who are laborers coming in at the eleventh hour, will be rewarded the same as our brothers and sisters who started early in the day. We both will receive full pay.

Here is the key: you will receive your pay if you

don't faint, quit, walk away, or throw in the towel.

Keep your eyes on the prize because Jesus is a great paymaster.

10
WILL GOD GET THE GLORY?

*The glory of the L*ORD *shall be revealed, And all flesh shall see it together; For the mouth of the L*ORD *has spoken.*

Isaiah 40:5, NKJV

Will God get the glory out of this? There have been times when our human nature rises up and begins to flex its muscles. We all have had those times when we were caught off guard. It may have been when someone said something that was rude or hurtful to us or when we were almost run off the road by an irresponsible driver.

You know, like the time when a cashier throws the change on the counter instead of placing it in your hand. Or what about the time you were accused of something that you didn't do and you tried with all your might to persuade your accusers that you were innocent, but to no avail? They not only didn't believe you; they began to tell others about the whole event. Maybe it's your family that has been the source of your test, and everything you have tried has failed to bring peace.

It doesn't matter where you are challenged—whether at home, at work, or even at church. It doesn't matter how or when you are challenged. It doesn't even matter whether the instrument was family, co-workers, friends, or co-laborers in the ministry. The only thing that really matters is: Will God get the glory out of this? Will the people involved and those who look on say to themselves or perhaps even aloud, "Wow!" because your reaction and response was so different than the average person on the street?

We cannot afford the luxury of allowing our personal feelings and our carnal nature to invade our lives. The power of the Holy Spirit will help us in those times when we really want to let go and give someone a piece of our mind. Will the glory of the Lord be revealed in us when we are acting just like people who do not have God in their lives?

In recent months, we have seen events that we could consider injustices based solely on the limited or biased information that we have received via the internet, CNN, Facebook, and other social media venues. The inhuman treatment of one person toward another is real and horrible, but we cannot let our emotions dictate our behavior or our comments.

We must be careful not to follow the crowd. The mob mentality gets you caught up in the spirit of these things, and you will find yourself speaking words that do not reflect a child of God. We are in this world but not of this world. I don't mean you should be quiet, but there is a response that should come from a child of God that helps usher in peace, comfort, direction, and healing.

We have to deal with difficult situations in life, but there must be one question that should guide our behavior, our reactions, our speech, and even our thought patterns. That question is: Will God get the glory out of this?

11
GOOD SHEPHERD

The L<small>ORD</small> is my shepherd; I shall not want.

Psalm 23:1, KJV

Psalm 23:1 is a powerful statement. The shepherd is one who watches out for the sheep. His main responsibility is for the care and welfare of the sheep.

The shepherd puts his needs second to the needs of the sheep. If the sheep are fitful and nervous, the shepherd finds out what is causing the unrest. The shepherd inspects the sheep every night to make sure they don't have injuries or anything that might interrupt their night's rest. The shepherd also checks the sheep's noses to ensure that flies have not laid eggs there. When flies lay their eggs in this warm moist place, the eggs hatch and the flies buzz in their noses. This causes the sheep to be so irritated that they literally bang their heads against trees. They have been known to knock themselves out!

The shepherd pours a special oil on the heads of the sheep that keeps the flies away. Knowing this makes Psalm 23:5, *"He anoints my head with oil"* take on a whole new meaning; doesn't it?

When we declare "The Lord is my shepherd," we must understand what is encompassed in such a statement. We have turned over our care to the Great Shepherd. It means that when there is an issue in our lives the Shepherd will be consulted, and He will in turn provide the best and most effective treatment.

So what is it that you are troubled about? What is it that you feel like you have to figure out all on your own? Cast all your cares on Him because He is the Good Shepherd and the Good Shepherd cares for His sheep (see John 10:11; 1 Peter 5:7).

The care of your children, the care of your family, the care of your extended family, and the needs of the community that affect you, the care of your mental health, the care of your emotional health, the care of your vision, the care of your destiny, the care of your entire life rests solely in the arms of the Good Shepherd.

Go ahead; you can trust the Good Shepherd. He will not let you down.

Only believe.

12
GOD'S GOODNESS

Truly God is good to Israel, even to such as are of a clean heart.

Psalm 73:1, KJV

You may be a natural descendant of Jacob or a spiritual son of Israel—either way, you can say, "God is good!" Making this statement is one of the ways to remind yourself that all things work together for good to those who love God (see Romans 8:28).

I know that events happen that make you wonder, "What has become of God?" On the surface, it might look bleak and hopeless. That is the time when you have to say, "Yes I see this; but God is good."
Whether it's your immediate family's issues, your extended family's problems, or even challenges in

the lives of families to whom you minister, there are things that can cause you to ask the questions: "Lord, where is the good in all this trouble?" or "Where is the good in all this pain?"

This world we live in is riddled with tragedy, earthquakes, sickness, disease, and unexplained hurts that happen on a daily basis. These things happen to people we know personally and to others that we hear about on the news. Yet, the Bible tells us that God is good. So what can we conclude from this?

Well, when there is pain, trouble, sickness, and trials on every hand, these problems do not change the character of God. He is still good. Life happens, but God is still good. Life is full of surprises, but God is still good. If you don't remind yourself of this on a regular basis, you may become bitter or frustrated.

There is a soothing comfort in knowing that although people may treat you badly, God is still good. It is gratifying to know that when friends turn their backs on you, God is still good. God is good when family members withhold their love and support for no apparent reason. God is good when you receive a diagnosis from the doctor that strikes fear in your heart.

There is something peaceful about knowing that

God's goodness will show up in the middle of your trial.
The Bible says, "Truly God is good to Israel . . . ." If you are in Christ, then everything—no matter what it is—will work together for your ultimate good.

13
ASCENSION

Let us therefore come boldly unto the throne of grace, that we may obtain mercy, and find grace to help in time of need.

Hebrews 4:16, KJV

Have you ever flown in a plane? As you ascend during takeoff, the pressure in the cabin changes and your ears are often affected. It's not that you can't hear at all, but your hearing is muffled and you feel the pressure. Some people suggest that chewing gum will help offset the effects of the change in cabin pressure on your ears. I have tried that, and it does seem to help.

In spite of the discomfort, you realize that the quickest way to get where you are going is by plane. So you can bear the discomfort when you know you are going somewhere. The same thing happens in the spirit world when we ascend in the Spirit through worship. The more aware we are of the presence of God and the more we draw near to Him, the more the atmosphere changes.

This experience is taking you somewhere. The spiritual man and the natural man are in two different worlds. The natural man cannot discern spiritual things. The spiritual world requires a spiritual sense. Sometimes, our senses are affected; spirit cries out to Spirit.

When you ascend into the spirit realm through prayer and worship, be prepared to write down what you see and hear. God will speak to you and give you answers that you never thought of before. He will show you things that you need to function more effectively on the ground. He will take you into His abode, where wonders and mighty works are the norm. This will seem foreign at first, but the more you ascend into His presence, the more acclimated you will become. You will adapt to the pressure of the cabin and make the necessary adjustments in your heart and mind.

These visitations to the realm of the Spirit are profitable because you will learn how to enter into your purpose on the earth. Another good thing about the spirit realm is that you will have access to the Almighty God. Whatever you need, He is there to provide. You are encouraged to "come boldly unto the throne of grace . . . ."

Even if the answer is "No!" you still have an audience with the King of kings. You will obtain grace to hear the proper answer for the situation and receive it because in this realm you know that the Father is all about doing what is good for you!

Denise S. Millben

14
HE HAS NOT FORGOTTEN YOU

For God is not unrighteous to forget your work and labour of love, which ye have shewed toward his name, in that ye have ministered to the saints, and do minister. And we desire that every one of you do shew the same diligence to the full assurance of hope unto the end.

Hebrews 6:10-11, KJV

God has not forgotten you!

What made you even think that God had forgotten you? Was it the disappointment that you felt when ministering to those that God has given you charge over? Maybe they misunderstood you, misinterpreted what you said, or just didn't want to follow your leading. Was it the embarrassment you felt when you thought you heard from God for the needs of the saints, but the results were not forth coming? Did you pray for one of the members who later died anyway?

Did you seek the Lord earnestly for the message to bring to the congregation; but they failed to appreciate it and even made statements like, "That message was not anointed" or "I didn't feel anything at all"? Did you discover that close friends were invited to someone's home, but you were excluded? Did you come up with a great plan and others took the credit for it? Have you ever been deliberately over looked and—fearing that you would appear carnal and petty if you mentioned it—you just grinned and bore it?

Could it be that you prayed for your child and the answer still has not manifested? Are your dreams unfulfilled? Do you not have enough money to pay your bills or do you have just a little left over? Or maybe there is something in your character that you know does not make the Lord smile, and you have prayed and prayed for that thing to leave. But it is still there; and you know that if left unchecked it could bring shame and harm to you and those you love and serve.

Pleading and crying does seem fruitless. Is God listening? Does He care? Can't He see you in this struggle?

It could be that we are not really seeing God in our everyday lives. In an attempt to get God to move, have we ignored the daily provision, help, strength, joy, peace, confidence, and victories that are downloaded into our lives daily? Thank you, Father.

Just because we have not seen the answer yet does not mean that the answer is "no"! So don't give up. God knows what is best for us all the time. Believe Hebrews 6:10 when it states that God is not unjust to forget your labor of love. He is recording everything you do and say while ministering to others. He will show you how much you are loved and how much He appreciates what you do on a daily basis.

Trust this one thing: He has not forgotten you.

15
WAIT FOR IT

For thus saith the LORD, *That after seventy years be accomplished at Babylon I will visit you, and perform my good word toward you, in causing you to return to this place.*

Jeremiah 29:1, KJV

In Jeremiah 29:1, the Lord is speaking through the prophet Jeremiah and He says, *"After your seventy years of captivity is over, I will visit you and perform my good word toward you and cause you to return to this place."* Wow! What a promise the children of Israel received from God. They had to go through a difficult experience, and they were not going to get out of their captivity early; but they did have God's promise that when the time was fulfilled they would return safely home.

Remember that the Bible was not written to us, but

it was written *for* us. So let's consider the spiritual application of this passage for our lives today. Many times, we are in severe tests and trials which feel like captivity. We desperately want to hear from God; but most of us do not want to hear God say, "You are going to remain in this trial longer." Instead, we want a word from God that says," In three days, you will be delivered." Or perhaps we just want to declare, "I'm out," or we want to seek out prophets who will prophesy our immediate deliverance.

But what happens when you do all of the above and there is still no change in your circumstances? This passage seems to say that God has an appointed time for you to come out of your captivity. What I believe is: there is a reason you are where you are. So in spite of the hardship, God is saying, "Hold on to my promise." God will not lie to you. He is saying, "Make a life and live until the prescribed time is over."

There is an old song that states, "You can't hurry God. You'll just have to wait. You've got to trust Him and give Him time. No matter how long it takes." But while you are waiting, live. Don't just sit and think, "Woe is me" or "Nobody knows the trouble I've seen." No! Repeat what the Lord told you. Tell it to yourself, and keep saying it until you believe it. God said you are coming out of this.

Did you know you can be—and must be—fruitful even in hard circumstances? The tree of righteousness will bud and blossom even in the most adverse situations. You are not alone, and you are not forgotten. The Word of God has gone forth. He said, "When your time of captivity is over, I will visit you and perform my good word toward you." Thank you, Jesus!

God has a plan. In due season, you are going to get a visitation from the Almighty God, and He is going to do something very good for you.

Wait for it, for it will surely come!

16
TRUTH TRUMPS FACTS

And ye shall know the truth, and the truth shall make you free.

John 8:32, KJV

The difference between fact and truth is this: facts are events that can be empirically proven, whereas truth is a state of being—a transcendent, fundamental, or spiritual reality. Facts are easy to believe because they are activated through the senses. However, Jesus said in John 8:31-32, *"If you abide in My word, you are My disciples indeed. And you shall know the truth, and the truth shall make you free"* (NKJV).

We are in the world, where the facts are so pronounced that it takes a conscious effort to push past the facts to embrace the truth. The problem often is that the facts are so much "in your face" that you find it difficult to grasp the truth and hold on to it. Facts are intimidating and they are enslaving. Facts constitute the enemy's version of the truth, and this version will prevail if we allow it. When facts are interpreted as truth, miracles are lost and blessings are forfeited.

Truth is actually more real than the things you can see, feel, taste, or touch. You must be careful not to elevate the facts over the truth. Truth transcends the earthly realm because it draws upon the unlimited power of God. As spiritual leaders in the house of God, it is important for us to buy (get and keep) the truth and not sell (or part with) it (see Proverbs 23:23). We live by the principles of the kingdom.

The facts say you are alone; but the truth is: God will never leave you nor forsake you (see Hebrews 13:5). The facts say that you will never come out of this pain or sorrow; but the truth is: *Yea, though you walk through the valley of the shadow of death, you shall fear no evil because He is with you and His rod and staff will comfort you (Psalm 23:4).* The facts say that this is a time to be fearful and nervous about the future; but the truth is: *There is no fear in love; but perfect love casts out fear because fear involves torment (see 1 John 4:18).*

Denise S. Millben

The truth is whatever God declares about a matter. We must speak the truth, walk in truth, declare the truth, worship in truth, obey the truth, and be established in truth.

What do we do when the facts tower over us like a giant helium balloon?

We know that truth trumps the facts every time.

17
PREPARE YOUR HEART

For Ezra had prepared his heart to seek the law of the LORD, and to do it, and to teach in Israel statutes and judgments.

Ezra 7:10, KJV

Ezra prepared his heart to seek the law of the Lord. How do you prepare your heart to seek the Lord? As a minister and servant of the Most High God, you might think, "That's a silly question." But in this busy life with all of its day-to-day events, we will need to prepare our hearts to seek the Lord. This scripture is not talking about just a casual glance, a chance encounter, or a quick "Hi and see you later, God." This is a deliberate time set aside to seek Him with a determined purpose.

As you ponder Ezra 7:10, I would like to offer a suggestion on how to prepare your heart. Some things just happen, whether good or evil. These things are not penciled in on the daily planner. They are unexpected events that require your time and attention. They are moments and events for which you cannot prepare.

There are also the events and occasions for which you can prepare. When you are expecting company, you prepare by getting extra food and beverages; you freshen up the guest room with clean sheets and the bathroom with fresh towels and a new bar of soap.

Similarly, preparing your heart to seek the Lord will require a few extra things that might not be in your normal routine. Turn off your cell phone. Choose a time when there will be fewer distractions—for example, early morning, late in the evening, after the children have gone to school, when the house is quiet, or during your lunch hour. Get music that will help you get into the worship realm—you know, into that special place with God. Get your Bible, pen, and paper. Inform your family that you do not want to be disturbed. Then go in and close the door.

When you get into the secret place, open your heart with pure honesty and devotion to God. Sweep out all the clutter from your heart. After all, this is a meeting with the King of kings. Worship and wait. Praise and continue to do this until you sense the presence of the King. Then listen to what He has to say. Write it down so you won't forget His instructions.

That is how you prepare your heart to seek the Lord. He is waiting for you to come!

18
LAUGH

A merry heart doeth good like a medicine: but a broken spirit drieth the bones.

Proverbs 17:22, KJV

Laughter is good medicine. In the ministry, it's easy to become solemn, somber, and even bitter. Many people expect ministers to be cold and serious; but I have found that laughter is good for you. When was the last time you laughed so hard that tears came to your eyes or your sides hurt?

Laughter is contagious. If you start to laugh at something, many times people around you will begin to smile even when they don't know what you are laughing about. I'm not talking about laughing at someone or something in a way that most people would consider being inappropriate or rude. I'm talking about laughing at a truly funny story that someone has shared or something funny you have read or heard. It's okay to laugh. It's okay to let others see you laugh.

I am terrible at telling jokes. I usually forget some important part of the story, like the punch line or something that makes the story even more humorous. It is okay to laugh at yourself, too. Don't take yourself too seriously. Laughter is something that we need more of. The Bible says it will do you good.

I have read several chapters of Erma Bombeck's travel log, *When You Look Like Your Passport Photo, It's Time to Go Home*. It is absolutely hilarious. Find humorous stories online. Read them and laugh, and then share them with someone else and laugh again. If you know of Christian comedians, spend the money and buy their CDs or DVDs, and just laugh and share them with a friend. I know there are times when you won't feel like laughing, and there are times when laughter is inappropriate; but that is not all the time. Did you know that you can be spiritual and laugh? It's true!

By the way, God has a great sense of humor. He will often cause us to laugh. Remember Abraham and Sarah? When the angel told Abraham that Sarah was going to have a baby in her old age, he laughed (see Genesis 17:16-17). When the angel told Sarah that she was going to bear a child, she laughed (see

Genesis 18:12-14). God will tell you things that can make you laugh—not in disbelief, but in total wonder. When you have a good laugh, you really feel better.

Go ahead have a good belly laugh—and help someone else laugh, too.

19
MY ANSWER IS YES

And Mary said, Behold the handmaid of the Lord; be it unto me according to thy word. And the angel departed from her.

Luke 1:38, KJV

Luke 1:38 records the statement that Mary, the mother of Jesus made when speaking to the angelic being named Gabriel. Mary's circumstances are very similar to our own in many ways. She was in an obscure town, her name was not in lights, and she had a common lifestyle—nothing big and fancy, nothing noteworthy. But one day, she had a conversation with an angelic being that changed her whole life.

Gabriel gives Mary information that would cause the average young girl to panic. The message was very clear. She was very young and perhaps had plans for her life that did not include being a mother at such a tender, young age. Nor did her plans include being the mother of the Messiah or being a mother out of wedlock. But this angelic declaration elicited a very powerful response from Mary. Her statement showed a level of trust in the message sent to her from God. In this one statement, she revealed her total dependence on the God of the universe. Within this one statement was wrapped all her fears, apprehensions, and future. She said, ". . . be it unto me according to thy word."

What does this story have to do with you? Well, you might be in a similar situation. You may be doing an obscure work in a remote corner of your town or city. You may feel like no one knows your name or even cares about you. You may be involved in the ministry, but no one knows who you really are. They only see the position you hold or the work you do; but who knows you deep inside? Who knows what you are called by God to become?

The Word of God might not come via an angelic being, but it might come in the form of a message preached on a Sunday night, that you know was for you. It was like the heavens opened up and the Word from God came right to you. And it didn't matter how many people were there; it was like the room contained only you and the Word.

So now here you are with this awesome Word from

Two Silver Trumpets

God, and what will be your response?

All I'm asking you to do is to make one statement like your sister Mary. Just say, "Be it unto me according to Your Word." That is telling God, "I don't have all the answers. I don't understand why You chose me. I don't know if I can do this. But here I am. I trust You to do with me as you like, and the outcome I leave in Your care!"

20
THE GREATNESS IN SILENCE

For thus saith the Lord GOD, the Holy One of Israel; In returning and rest shall ye be saved; in quietness and in confidence shall be your strength: and ye would not.

Isaiah 30:15, KJV

Have you ever been in a wonderful spiritual atmosphere where something awesome is taking place? The air is supercharged with joy and peace. Tranquility and almost a sense of euphoria are permeating the room. This is a time for the holy hush. It's a time when no words are needed. This is when you want to soak in every nuance of what is taking place. You want to savor these precious moments and carefully tuck them away in your memory bank to rehearse them another time.

Then it happens. Someone releases words that are totally out of order and they ruin the moment. It's like when you are experiencing a beautiful worship time with the Lord and someone says, "I wonder what restaurant we are going to when this is over." Really? Perhaps it's a little less tacky than that. They might say, "We are all out of tissue. I need to remember to get some the next time I go to the store." OMG! That is what happens when people are not comfortable with silence. They just can't be quiet and allow the moment to come and leave without verbal input. While in the presence of God, it's okay to quietly take in the moment without speaking.

On the Mount of Transfiguration, something spectacular took place (see Matthew 17:1-9). Jesus was speaking to the prophets of old, Elijah and Moses. As the disciples watched, Jesus' clothes turned whiter than snow and His face began to glisten. The moment was supernatural. However, Peter was uncomfortable with the sights and the silence, so he spoke out of his soul. In supernatural moments, the natural mind can hardly comprehend the spiritual. Peter felt that he needed to say something, so he did: "It is good for us to be here." Now, this vocal seal of approval was not so bad. But he should have stopped there. Instead, he continued to speak and ruined the moment by saying, "Let's build a monument for all three" (see v. 4).

Take a quick lesson from Peter. When something supernaturally special is happening, quietly consent and let it soak into your spirit. It's okay to remain quiet for a while. There may be more that needs to be revealed, demonstrated, or downloaded. In this fast-paced world, special times with the Lord should be valued and cherished.

21
I MADE IT

Now God himself and our Father, and our Lord Jesus Christ, direct our way unto you. And the Lord make you increase and abound in love one toward another, and toward all men, ever as we do toward you.

1 Thessalonians 3:11-12, KJV

Wow! What a powerful scripture. First Thessalonians 3:11 says that God is not going to entrust the task of directing your way to any other. This job of directing your life is so important that He is going to see to it Himself. You see, this business of being on the right path is vital to arriving at the right destination. If you get on the highway headed north and your destination is east, you will never reach it even if you drive all day and all night long. Why? Because your direction is wrong.

The direction God has for you is too important to

leave it in the hands of anyone else, so He Himself is going to direct your way. This is to ensure that you arrive at your proper destination within a specific timeframe and with everything you need to be successful when you get there.

God's path for your life leads to increase and an abundance of love (see v. 12). You will not only love others, but you will also love yourself. That is not a self-centered or ego-boosting statement. Before you can love others properly, you must love yourself.

Sometimes there will be long stretches when you might not see anything to tell you that you are on the right track. When you are traveling your life's path, there may come a time when you might wonder if this is the right road simply because it feels wrong. Don't make the mistake of getting off at the next exit just because the road may be bumpy or dark with only a few markers to point you in the right direction.

Don't rely on feelings. If you didn't get off the road, then it is right no matter how you feel. You didn't miss your turn. Stay the course and travel on. If you haven't deviated from the path, then it is the right road. Stay on the path because this path has been chosen by God, and it is right.

Every now and then say, "Thank you, Jesus for this

path." Praise is always in order. Even when you don't understand, praise the Lord for His Word. Don't think for a moment that you are drifting down life's path without a friend or a guide. The Lord Himself will direct your way. What a comfort. Praise the Lord!

This is a custom-made way for you. Stay on the path; and when you arrive at your destination, you will be able to say with a loud voice, "Thank you, Jesus. I made it!"

22
LOVE IS STRONG

Owe no man anything, but to love one another: for he that loveth another hath fulfilled the law.

Romans 13:8, KJV

Make a plan to become debt free. Especially all those credit card debits you owe. I know that is so convenient to have a card and spend money that you don't have on bargains and sales that might be gone by the time you actually have the money. Been there done that! But as I took another look at some of the debt we were in, I realized that debt was a cruel task master. Cracking the whip and making us bow. It was a distraction from the things God wanted us to do. Many times we felt the prompting of the Holy Spirit to give beyond what we had in our wallets, but debt began to scream in our ears, "you better not give, you better not write that check," because we had a J.C. Penny's bill due, and a Visa,

Lazarus, Carson, H.H. Gregg, and others. It is difficult to obey the voice of the Lord when the spirit of mammon is speaking loud and clear. We had become slaves to debt. Perhaps you can identify with me on this. You know that I'm right. We learned the hard way. We never had to file bankruptcy but we sure thought about it and came dangerously close.

Listen, the Lord is waking the church up to many things and debt is one of them. Let's face it. We have been living above our means in many situations. I'm not talking about unforeseen medical bills or other expenses that just happen in life. I'm talking about willful debt. You know those companies that charge outrageous interest. We often find ourselves emotionally buying things based on its attraction to our eyes and willful desires. We must stop. There are things that you will have to buy immediately without having a chance to think about it. Some things will require your attention, like a flat tire. It happens suddenly and you have to take care of it. But there are other things that capture your time and money and prevent you from freely giving your time ,but the task master says you need to work overtime just to make ends meet.

It is not too late to turn things around. This is a good time to look at all your bills and begin a strategy to pay them off. Mr. Dave Ramsey has a great program to help people get debt free. You need to invest in your future. Enroll right away. Get rid of your credit cards. Apply for a debit card that you can use if you don't like carrying cash. You can use it when traveling for hotels, airline tickets, making purchases online and making payments this way you can keep up with your spending. The time is now. I know you might feel like, "If only it were that easy." Well, let me tell you, easy or not, you must make a sincere effort to get out from under the debt load as quickly as possible. Early in our ministry I never really saw anything wrong with making debt outside of the normal things we use credit for, i.e. home, cars etc. but let me say this is not the plan God has for His children.

This is something you can take to our heavenly Father in prayer and ask for his help and guidance to better fulfill His plan for your life. God is able to show you just how to do it. He is able and so are You!

23
TAKE A STAND

Stand therefore, having your loins girt about with truth, and having on the breastplate of righteousness.

Ephesians 6:14, KJV

We live in a time when standing for something that is unpopular is rare. We seem to be forced to comply with the status quo or suffer ridicule. We have a term for it: being politically correct. This means don't say anything that would be considered offensive, judgmental, corrective, or challenging.

But I am reminded of some people in the Bible who seized the opportunity to represent their God. We refer to them as "the three Hebrew boys" (see Daniel 3). They did not have to say anything; they just stood for what they believed was right while everyone else in the nation bowed. That took commitment and resolve. They were not patted on the back and encouraged. Instead, they were arrested and punished.

In this hour, to be politically correct could very well mean that you must go against God's Word. But as a leader, where does your allegiance lie? The line is clearly drawn between the Lord and the enemy, and the space between the two is getting wider every day. You may believe that the Word of God is true; but when it comes to standing for it publicly, you will need resolve in your heart. God's kingdom is an everlasting kingdom, and those who are subject to His kingdom must live by its laws.

I just read an article about the owners of Hobby Lobby standing for what they believe. Maintaining their position could cost them the family business that has been in existence for forty years. They have a firm belief system, and they are representing the kingdom of God in this matter. They are drawing from the resolve they held long before this issue came up. This commitment is what they use to represent their faith in God.

The task that the church and its leaders are faced with may seem enormous, daunting, and even nigh to impossible; but, actually, it's the opposite. Representing God is doable when you have a resilient commitment to God. You have to make up your mind in advance. We have been assured that God will be with us in the fire.

The Hebrew boys said, "*We don't know if the Lord will deliver us; but this we know: even if He doesn't, we will not bow*" *(see vv. 16-18). God has not given us the spirit of fear but of power, love, and a sound mind (2 Timothy 1:7).*

Thank God for the power to represent Him well!

24
A CRY OF FAITH

*This poor man cried, and the L*ORD *heard him, and saved him out of all his troubles.*

Psalm 34:6, KJV

Sometimes, you will cry. That's all right because God created tears and He gave us different emotions— one of which is sadness. But one thing He did not give us is despair. So if you need to cry, it's all right; but do not cry in despair. Despair is misery, desolation, and hopelessness. With Christ, that is never your true condition.

There was a man in the Bible who was blind (see Matthew 10:46-52). We aren't told much about him other than his condition and his name: blind Bartimaeus, the son of Timaeus. From the story, we can deduce that he was inquisitive, knowledgeable, and resourceful. This poor man cried, and his cry got

Jesus' attention. There is only one cry that can get God's attention—that is the cry of faith.

This man cried, *"Jesus, thou son of David, have mercy on me" (v. 47).* When this man cried, Jesus heard him, stopped, and sent for him. The cry of faith can get Jesus to stop and move on your behalf. When the people told blind Bartimaeus that Jesus was calling for him, "Who me?" was not his response. He threw his garments aside because he had heard from the Master. Those garments were an indication of his current condition as a beggar.

When Jesus calls for you, this is the lesson you need to take from this blind man: Cast off the garments that represent the situation you are in. Get ready. There is about to be a change. Your blindness is only because you can't see your way out of this situation, condition, problem, or circumstance. Other people may have pity on you, but pity is not what you need. You need Jesus to stop and do something about this. The garments of your current condition are dirty, torn, and smelly. They reek of the situation. Cast those garments off and see what Jesus clothes you with.

So, it is okay to cry. But make sure that you are crying in faith to the only one who can help in the time of need. Faith in Jesus Christ will make all the difference in the type of crying you do. You are not crying just because you are hurting. You are crying

Denise S. Millben

to get Jesus' attention—because He is the only one who can make things better for you.

The cry of faith is the cry that makes Jesus stop!

25
GRACIOUS DEALINGS

I'll make a list of GOD's gracious dealings, all the things GOD has done that need praising. All the generous bounties of GOD, his great goodness to the family of Israel—Compassion lavished, love extravagant.

Isaiah 63:7, MSG

Go ahead; make your list. You really shouldn't have to rack your brain to come up with an impressive list because God's gracious dealings should be right in the forefront of your mind.

Start with just a few minutes ago. What about last night, yesterday, and all day long? You went about your daily duties and completed many, if not all, of them. You thought that you were the one who was getting the job done, but this was the "gracious dealings" of the Lord in your life. It may take a while to list everything; but as you go through your day, you can thank God for His generous bounty—the compassion that He has lavished on you and those around you.

Now take some time to say, "thank you" after each item you listed. I know you thank Him for major help, but what about for getting up this morning with health and strength? Or what about merely getting up at all? What about thanking Him that you were not a victim of the home invasions that happen with increasing frequency? Thank God for what He has kept away from you, your family, and your friends. The old saints used to say, "Thank God for protection from danger, both seen and unseen."

Thank God for forgiveness. There are times when you can't believe you have done something so crazy. You are embarrassed and find it hard to ask God for forgiveness, but there He stands ready to lavish His compassion upon you and forgive you. He even prompts you to forgive yourself! What a mighty God! Then think about His extravagant (more than usual, necessary, or proper; lacking in moderation, balance, and restraint) love. God's love for us is more than usual, more than necessary, more than what is proper. Oh my goodness. What a mighty God!

Thank you, Lord for pouring that kind of goodness on us this day. When you are tempted to look at circumstances that are not good, you might get bogged down in the present situation. So pull out your list and begin to rehearse God's gracious dealings with you, and you will get a different perspective on the condition you are in right now.

"Because thy lovingkindness is better than life, my lips shall praise thee" (Psalm 63:3, KJV).

My list of God's gracious dealings:
_____
_____
_____
_____
_____
_____
_____
_____
_____
_____
_____
_____
_____
_____
_____
_____
_____
_____
_____
_____
_____
_____
_____
_____

26
GET ON FIRE

And whatsoever ye do, do it heartily, as to the Lord, and not unto men.

Colossians 3:23, KJV

What is your passion? What is the activity that you could do all day long and not grow weary of doing? What is the thing that you desire—that you are hungry and thirsty for? What is that thing that makes you smile when you think about getting involved with it?

Passion is a strong feeling that can motivate you to do some incredible things. In ministry, you need passion. There are parts of ministry that you might not have a passion for, but there needs to be at least one thing that you love deeply in your soul. What is that something that brings you joy?

Consider your passion. Remember the times when it was so easy for you to stay up late and arise early in the morning to do something? Where did that drive and love go? If you have lost it, ask God to restore it. You need passion to fulfill the will of God with ease.

Without passion, even the easiest things can become hard and arduous. Your passion can get buried under the mundane tasks that need doing but are very inconsequential in the overall scheme of things. If you feel buried under the weight of the ministry, you need to get back to your passion. Ask God to give you that smile on the inside that comes when you are doing what you really love.

Did you know that your passion can become contagious? People who are passionate about anything can cause others to become passionate about something. It doesn't have to be the same thing. When you see a passionate person, you get inspired. It's like you catch on fire, and then you ignite someone else. There are so many dry people who have lost their thirst for life. Then there are those who have had a fire, but they allowed someone to pour water on it. They need to be reignited.

What fires you up? Ponder that thing and the possibilities that it poses. Get on fire, and let it put a glow back in your eyes. Let your fire or passion pass on to someone else; and before you know it, those within your sphere of influence will be passionate and on fire. The world needs positive, passionate people.

27
RESTORATION

But ye, brethren, be not weary in well doing.

2 Thessalonians 3:13. KJV

The admonition "don't lose heart" means "don't give up" or "don't lose confidence." Don't allow discouragement to rest upon you. Continue believing that the Lord will come through and deliver you. The promise from Almighty God is that He will direct your way. I know you have been waiting for the Lord to answer that special prayer that you have been praying for a long time, but don't lose heart.

Read the Word of God and see the many examples He left for us that will encourage us in times like these. The children of Israel were waiting for a deliverer. When the time was right, the Lord raised up Moses to bring them out of bondage (see Exodus

3). Don't lose heart. The same God who delivered the children of Israel out of a hostile environment will deliver you.

Another example that God has given to help us is of a woman named Rahab (see Joshua 2). Rahab was a prostitute, but she knew about the great God Jehovah and spared the lives of the spies. They, in turn, spared her life and the lives of her family. The entire city was destroyed, but Rahab and her family were delivered by God. The Lord will bring you out. He will answer your prayers, so don't lose heart.

There are blessings waiting, and they will come through love. Perfect love casts out fear (see 1 John 4:18). Any fear that you are praying in vain will be cast out. Don't lose heart. God Himself will help you.

I Thessalonians 3:11-12 says, *"Now God himself and our Father, and our Lord Jesus Christ, direct our way unto you. And the Lord make you to increase and abound in love one toward another, and toward all men, even as we do toward you" (KJV).* Reread the words: "God himself . . . direct our way . . . and make you to increase. . . ." This scripture suggests that the Lord is not sending the angels to assist in this task, but He is going to do this Himself.

This day, I speak a restoration of your faith toward God and your trust that He won't fail you. There is an old song written by Civilla D. Martin that says,

"Be not dismayed whate'er betide, God will take care of you; Beneath His wings of love abide, God will take care of you." Don't lose heart, give up, become discouraged, or lose confidence. Instead, be sure and know that God will take care of you.

28
WAIT ON HIM

This I recall to my mind, therefore have I hope. It is of the LORD's mercies that we are not consumed, because his compassions fail not. They are new every morning: great is thy faithfulness. The LORD is my portion, saith my soul; therefore will I hope in him. The LORD is good unto them that wait for him, to the soul that seeketh him. It is good that a man should both hope and quietly wait for the salvation of the LORD.

Lamentations 3:21-26, KJV

Waiting. Is that easy for you? If we were to take a poll, I would suspect that many people would rate waiting as unpleasant, difficult, or even impossible! How about you?

Well, I guess it depends on what you are waiting for. Have you ever been tempted to change lanes at the bank or in the grocery store? Then, when you got into a new line, the line that you left started to move. If you are waiting for your turn to place an order at Taco Bell when someone ahead of you has four separate orders with special instructions on each one, that could be considered a time to exercise your patience. How about waiting for the bank's approval of your mortgage when you must vacate your apartment soon? Waiting could bring some apprehension or become quite a test. What about waiting for a document to arrive in the mail that will seal the deal for a great job opportunity? Waiting with expectancy can be a challenge. Waiting can sometimes produce great anticipation, like waiting for the birth of your first child. Yes, you have to wait, but at the end of your waiting, you are going to receive the prize.

What about waiting on God to bring the answer to your prayers? Waiting for God might be easier when you are the only one who knows about a particular need. But what do you do as a leader when the whole group you are leading is looking to you for the answer?

What you need to know is that waiting is not fruitless. You are doing something when you are waiting. So while you're waiting and all eyes are on you, meditate on Lamentation 3:21-26.
God will come through. Don't be pushed or pressured into going ahead of the leading of the Lord. Remember, the Lord is good unto them that

wait for Him. Don't rush out and do something rash just so people will see you doing something. Waiting *is* doing something.

Wait on the Lord, and He shall strengthen your heart. Wait, I say, on the Lord (see Psalm 27:14).

29
GOD OUR AVENGER

Beloved, do not avenge yourselves, but rather give place to wrath; for it is written, "Vengeance is Mine, I will repay," says the Lord.

Romans 12:19, NKJV

Perhaps things have happened to you that are unfair, dishonest, cruel, unlawful, immoral, and just plain wicked. These experiences can become your captors if you spend your waking hours thinking of how you are going to avenge yourself. The disbelief and the horror of what was done can keep you imprisoned in your mind. It can make you bitter and vengeful.

It's okay to cry out for God to avenge you against your enemies. However, even though your enemy has a face and a name, that face is not your real enemy. Your enemy is that evil spirit behind the person—the spirit that prompted them to do or say what they did.

Listen, if you have been targeted by evil spirits, then nothing you do in the flesh will change anything. But when you cry out to your heavenly Father asking Him to avenge you, Romans 12:19 says that vengeance is God's; He will repay. The issue is not the faithfulness of the Lord God Almighty. The issue is whether you will be persistent in your supplication. Isaiah 62:6-7 says, *"I have set watchmen upon thy walls, O Jerusalem, which shall never hold their peace day nor night: ye that make mention of the Lord, keep not silence, And give him no rest, till he establish, and till he make Jerusalem a praise in the earth"* (KJV).

Spiritually you are partakers of the promises given to Israel. So as a personal application of Isaiah 62:6-7, you can cry day and night and give your Father no rest until He avenges you and makes you an object of praise in the earth. In other words, you should continue to pray until God lets others see how He takes care of people who bother you.

The Lord is like the big brother on the playground when bullies are bothering you. You get very bold when you know that your brother will take care of the situation. Luke 18:8-9 says, *"And shall God not avenge His own elect who cry out day and night to Him, though He bears long with them? I tell you that He will*

Two Silver Trumpets

avenge them speedily."

This is a matter of turning things over to God and believing that He can—and will—handle your situation. It is a freeing way to live. You don't have to fight your own battles. You don't have to track down your enemies. God's got them in His sights, and He will do what needs to be done in every case.

God sees and He knows all. You can trust Him and rest in that assurance, and walk away from each occurrence in liberty.

30
THE LAND OF FAITH

For I am not ashamed of the gospel of Christ: for it is the power of God unto salvation to everyone that believeth; to the Jew first, and also to the Greek. For therein is the righteousness of God revealed from faith to faith: as it is written, The just shall live by faith.

Romans 1:16-17, KJV

Every believer in Jesus Christ has faith. To come to God, you must have faith (see Hebrews 11:6). Perhaps you have exercised faith in the Word of God to bring about a desired result in a given situation. Then there is the faith to heal the sick; it is a faith that all believers have but not all believers utilize. Many times we, as believers, muster up the faith to do something that is pressing on our hearts; but that level of faith comes only with the urgent need and lifts when the need is gone.

I am inviting you to begin an adventure with me into a place I have discovered. It is the place that is accessible to us; and in this place there are no limits. Yes, that's right, no limits. This place is where you can say to this mountain, "Be thou removed," and it will have to obey you.

One day, I was watching a television series called *Stargate SG-1.* In one scene, I saw a blue oval shimmering portal. That portal was a point of entry to another location. You could arrive just by going through the opening. Right then and there, the Spirit of the Lord began to speak to me. He said that there is a place that you can enter that takes you into another dimension where the impossible becomes possible—a place where you can take God at His Word. It is not far from us, but we often miss it in our walk with God. It's a place that I call "The Land of Faith."

We have had visits into the land of faith under stressful situations, but I'm not talking about visiting in the land, I'm talking about living there. I'm talking about changing your address and moving from the land of our nativity—which is full of worry, doubt, fear, and many other enemies of faith—into a land that is full of promise.

Go ahead and jump into the land of faith; and when you get there, plant gardens and build a house and put out your mailbox. This is an exciting place. There is so much to learn and see and experience. You will change your language. You will no longer say, "I can't" or "I hope so." No, you will use the language of faith—like "I can do all things through Christ who strengthens me" (see Philippians 4:13).

God wants us to live here because He is moved by faith. Now, I must warn you that there will be times when you find yourself jumping back to the land of sight; but as soon as you realize where you are, just self-correct and jump right back into the land of faith. You may have to do this several times before you jump and never look back.

This land of faith is not heaven. So there will be challenges in the land, but you will overcome them all. God has not given us the spirit of fear, but of power and love and a sound mind (see 2 Timothy 1:7).

There is so much to see and do in the land of faith. You enter through the Word, and you stay there by speaking the Word. This is how the just shall live.

To request Denise Millben for your upcoming conference, retreat or event, please contact her at:

Christ Temple Global Ministries
654 N. Jefferson St.
Muncie, IN 47305
(765) 587-4189

www.ingramcontent.com/pod-product-compliance
Lightning Source LLC
LaVergne TN
LVHW051517070426
835507LV00023B/3161